ETHNIC CHRONOLOGY SERIES
NUMBER 2

The Blacks in America
1492–1977

A Chronology & Fact Book

Fourth Revised Edition

Compiled and edited by
Irving J. Sloan

1977
OCEANA PUBLICATIONS, INC.
DOBBS FERRY, NEW YORK

Library of Congress Cataloging in Publication Data

Sloan, Irving J.
    Blacks in America, 1492-1975.

    (Ethnic chronology series; no. 2)
    First-2d ed. published under title: The American
Negro; a chronology and fact book.
    Bibliography: p.
    Includes index.
    SUMMARY: A chronology of blacks in America with such
additional lists of information as major Afro-American
organizations and publications, libraries with black
history and literature collections, and a statistical
abstract of Afro-American economic and social status.
    1. Afro-Americans—History—Chronology. 2. Afro-Americans.
[1. Afro-Americans—History—Chronology. 2. Afro-Americans]
I. Title. II. Series.
E185.S57   1976   973'.04'96073   76-5910
ISBN 0-379-00524-7

JUL   81

Manufactured in the United States of America

To Eric Rothschild,
friend and colleague,
and a teacher's teacher
of black history.

TABLE OF CONTENTS

INTRODUCTION

No one can measure the influence or the impact of history on the minds of men. It is certain, however, that the kind of historical treatment --or the lack of it--which the Negro in America has received under the guise of "historical scholarship" has made no small contribution in establishing and perpetuating one of our society's most serious problems: racial discrimination. For the fact is that by omission and commission the history of the American Negro has served to reinforce notions among whites of their superiority and among Negroes of their inferiority.

Dr. John Hope Franklin has distinguished "between what has actually happened and what those who have written history have said has happened." He goes on to hail the changes that have occurred in the writing of the history of the Negro in recent years. Indeed, these changes are even more dramatic than the very events themselves that the writers have been describing. "For the first time in the history of the United States, there is a striking resemblance between what historians are writing and what has actually happened in the history of the American Negro. "

This small volume presents chronologically and factually the broad sweep of American Negro history. There is no attempt here to amplify or to interpret. For the most part, a book of this nature serves as a quick, handy and, hopefully, reliable reference work. Having located a person or event of interest, the reader can seek out the full story in any number of books which are filling the shelves of literature on Negro life and history.

Compact as the present work is, one can yet come to have an appreciation of the background and the contribution of the Negro in American life by surveying its contents.

The reader will learn at once that Negro history in America does not begin with the first cargo of slaves which was landed in Jamestown in 1619. It begins with the very beginning of American history with the coming of the European explorers. Scholars, indeed, contend that Columbus' pilot was a Negro. But in any case there is no historical doubt that the discoverer of the Pacific Ocean, Balboa, brought with him 30 Negroes whose assistance was invaluable. Cortez was accompanied by a Negro, who, finding in his rations of rice some grains of wheat, planted them as an experiment and thereby introduced wheat raising in the Western Hemisphere. Negroes participated in the exploration of Guatemala and the conquest of

Chile, Peru, and Venezuela. Negroes were with Ayllon in 1526 in his expedition from the Florida Peninsula northward and took a part in the establishment of the settlement of San Miguel, near what is now Jamestown, Virginia. Negroes accompanied Navarez on his ill-fated adventure in 1526 and continued with Cabeza de Vaca, his successor, through what is now the southwestern part of the United States. There Estevancio, a Negro, discovered Cibola, "the seven cities" of the Zuni Indians. Matthew A. Henson, the last to appear in the role of explorer, was chosen by Commodore Perry to accompany him to the North Pole.

The first important contribution of the Negro to the development of America was labor. First as indentured servants and then after being debased to the status of slaves, Negroes supplied the demand for labor demanded by the expansion of trade in the commercial revolution of the modern era. Negroes cleared the forests of the Southland, drained the swamps, prepared the soil for the production of its staples, and dug from the earth nuggets of precious metals. In all sections of America appeared Negro mechanics and artisans, using the skill which was natural to the African even in his native land. These Negro workers shod horses, cast farming implements, made vehicles, constructed boats, and built railroads.

At the same time the Negro showed inventive genius in producing labor-saving devices. Negroes assisted Eli Whitney in his experiments with the cotton gin and McCormick with his reaper. James Forten perfected a machine for handling sails; Henry Blair patented two corn harvesters; Granville T. Woods stimulated industry with his electrical patents; Elijah McCoy brought machinery nearer to perfection with his lubricating devices; Norbert Rillieux revolutionized the manufacture of sugar with his vacuum pan; and Jan E. Matzeliger revolutionized the shoe industry with the lasting device for making shoes with machinery.

While helping to develop the country, the Negro has done his share in defending it. As this Chronology relates again and again, the Negro has acquitted himself with honor in all American wars. They served with the Colonial forces and helped shape the destiny of America. They followed the British standard during the Seven Years War until Montcalm was vanquished by Wolfe on the Plains of Abraham, thereby making English institutions possible in America.

In the American Revolution some 5,000 Negroes fought on the American side with distinction. Negroes were honored as heroes at Bunker Hill and Stony Point. George Washington praised the Negro soldier. Even more fulsome praise was given the Negro soldier by Andrew Jackson after the Battle of New Orleans in 1815; for during the War of 1812 Negroes also fought with impressive distinction.

The great social and political issue of the years following was the question of slavery in 19th century America. Negro newspapers, such as Freedom's Journal and Walker's Appeal, and Negro leaders, such as Douglass, Garnet, Ward and Pennington, were in the forefront of the abolition movement which brought the nation in the direction of freedom and equality for all.

The Civil War began as a war to save the Union and succeeded also in destroying slavery. Again the Negro participated in promoting democracy in America. Over two hundred thousand Negroes fought with the Union forces. History confirms the deeds of heroism performed by individual Negro soldiers as well as the significant contribution they made to final victory in terms of numbers alone.

The achievements of the Negro in the theatre, literature, music and the arts through the present day are too familiar to warrant recapitulation here. His role in the wars this country has fought and still fights in this century are also well-known if not always well-recognized. Our Chronology here records all this.

What is perhaps most significant and exciting is to note how in the last decade the events and the people involved in present-day Negro history in the making are largely related to the Negroes' struggle on their own behalf for full equality in American society. Coupled with this series of events is the ever-increasing "firsts" among Negroes--the "first" Negro to appear with the Metropolitan Opera; the "first" Negro to enter the Major Leagues in baseball; the "first" Negro to enter a Southern state university, and on and on and on.

And as we see Negroes enter politics and public office our knowledge of Negro history will serve as reassuring evidence that they bring to American public life a background of positive achievements when given the opportunity. During the Reconstruction, contrary to biased and now generally repudiated "history, "the Negro gave a good account of himself as a citizen and as a statesman. The majority of the Negro leaders of that day advocated high ideals. The participation of the Negro in the affairs of the Government was denounced and opposed from the very beginning; but despite the mire of corruption into which the Negroes were drawn by the white men who profited at the expense of the freedmen, the Negro demonstrated his capacity for citizenship and his right to all the honors within the gift of the United States. Indeed, the Negro had never imposed upon government such colossal evidences of corruption and scandal as the "credit mobilier, " the "whiskey ring, " the "Tweed ring" and many others which were recorded throughout the country during the same period.

It is the very aim of a book like this to make some small contribution toward setting down the historical achievements and therefore historical truths concerning such a large part of our American people, the Negro. In proposing this, one need not suggest that we learn less about the great leaders and episodes already recognized and honored in American history. It only means that we include in our knowledge the role of the Negro in our history. Having that knowledge will give us the understanding that the Negroes' long "advance from slavery to freedom and from freedom to equality has significantly involved and affected the lives of millions of Americans of all races and all generations." Such an understanding will make it possible to accept Negro fellow citizens as equals-and this, after all, is what the most critical issue of our democratic society is all about today.

CHRONOLOGY

CHRONOLOGY

1442   First African slave brought to Lisbon, Portugal.

1492   Pedro Alonzo Nino, said by many scholars to have been a Negro, arrived with Columbus as one of his pilots. Oct. 12.

1513   Balboa's expedition to the Pacific included thirty Blacks who were instrumental in clearing the way between two oceans. April.

1517   Bishop Las Casas influenced the Spanish government to allow Spaniards to import twelve Negroes each to encourage immigration to the New World.

1526   The first slave revolt took place in the first United States settlement which contained slaves--an area in present-day South Carolina. April 22.

1538   Estevanico (Little Stephen), a Black explorer, led expedition from Mexico and discovered Arizona and New Mexico.

1539   Blacks accompanied De Soto on his journey to the Mississippi.

1540   The second settler in the state of Alabama was a Black who was with De Soto's expedition. Liking the land, he settled among the Indians.

1562   John Hawkins carried slaves from Portuguese Africa to Spanish America.

1565   Blacks were with Mendez in founding St. Augustine, Florida.

1619   A Dutch ship anchored at Jamestown, Virginia, with a cargo of "twenty Negras"--thus began Black history in English America. Aug.

1620   The first public school for Negroes and Indians in Virginia was established.

1624   William Tucker was the first Black child born and baptized in English America at Jamestown, Virginia.

1638   First Black slaves were brought into New England.

1641   Massachusetts was the first colony to recognize slavery as a legal institution.

1644   Marriage of Antony van Angola and Lucie d'Angola was the first in Negro life to be recorded in America on Manhattan Island.

1645   Voyage of the <u>Rainbowe</u>, the first American slave ship.

1661   First individual petition of a Black for his freedom addressed to the colony of New Netherland was granted.

1662   Virginia enacted a statute making slavery hereditary, following the status of the mother.

1663   The first major slave rebellion in colonial America took place in Gloucester, Virginia.

1664   Maryland passed a law preventing marriages between English women and Negroes; several of the colonies followed suit soon thereafter.

1671   Maryland passed Act declaring that conversion of slaves to Christianity did not affect their slave status.

1672   The King of England chartered the Royal African Company which came to dominate the world slave trade.

1688   Quakers of Germantown, Pennsylvania, made the first formal protest against slavery in the Western hemisphere. Feb. 18.

1704   Elias Nau, a Frenchman, opened the first school for Blacks in New York City.

1705   Virginia enacted a law permitting owners to list people as property.

1712   Early slave revolt in New York City. April 7.
Pennsylvania passed first legislation to prevent importation of slaves.

1713   Anthony Benezet, a teacher of Blacks and leading abolitionist in Pennsylvania, born.

1715   Francisco Xavier de Luna Victoria was the first Black to become bishop in America (Panama).

1720	Jupiter Hammon of Long Island, the first Black American writer, was born in Africa.
1731	Benjamin Banneker, colonial mathematician and astronomer, was born near Baltimore, Maryland. Nov. 9.
1733	Samuel Sewall published the first anti-slavery tract which appeared in the colonies, "The Selling of Joseph."
1741	A serious slave revolt in New York City resulted in the hanging of eighteen Blacks. March-April.
1745	A Black, Jean Baptiste Pointe Du Saible, who established a trading post which later became the city of Chicago, was born in Haiti.
1746	Toussaint L'ouverture, revolutionary leader of Haiti, born. May 20.
1747	Absalom Jones, first Black minister ordained in America, born a slave in Sussex, Delaware.
1748	Prince Hall, successful businessman and founder of Negro Free Masonry, born.
1750	Crispus Attucks, first martyr of the American Revolution, escaped from his master in Framingham, Massachusetts. Sept. 30.
1753	Scipio Moorhead, earliest known Black artist, born. Lemuel Haynes, first Negro to serve as pastor in white congregation in the United States, born. July 18.
1756	John Woolman began his campaign against slavery. May 12.
1758	Frances Williams, first Black college graduate in Western hemisphere, published Latin poems. April 17.
1759	Paul Cuffee, business leader and philanthropist, born. Jan. 17.
1760	Richard Allen, founder and bishop of the African Methodist Church, born a slave near Philadelphia. Feb. 14.
1761	Phillis Wheatley, poetess of the American Revolutionary period, arrived in Boston harbor on a slave ship.

1761   Jupiter Hammon published "An Evening Thought." Dec. 15.

1762   James Derham, the first recognized Black medical doctor in
                America, born in Philadelphia.

1768   Rev. James Varick, first Superintendent and bishop of the
                African Methodist Episcopal Zion Church, born in New York
                City.

1770   Crispus Attucks was the first of the five men to be killed in
                the Boston Massacre. March 5.
                Anthony Benezet opened school for Negroes in Philadelphia.
                June 28.

1772   Lord Mansfield handed down his decision in the Somerset
                case against the existence of slavery on English soil. This
                case stimulated requests for legislative action against slav-
                ery in New England. June 22.

1773   George Leile and Andrew Bryan organized the first Negro
                Baptist Church in Savannah, Georgia.
                Bill Richmond, father of modern prize fighting, born in
                Staten Island.
                Jean Baptiste Point du Saible, first permanent settler in
                Chicago, purchased the house and land of Jean Baptiste Millet
                at "Old Peoria Fort."
                Massachusetts slaves petitioned the state legislature for
                their freedom. Jan. 6.

1774   Continental Congress voted an agreement not to import any
                slaves after December 1.

1775   Bejamin Franklin was elected president upon the establish-
                ment of the first abolition society organized in America by
                the Quakers in Philadelphia. April 14.
                Black soldiers fought in the Battle of Bunker Hill. Peter
                Salem, who shot down Major Pitcairn, was one of the heroes
                of the day. June 17.
                Continental Congress passed a resolution barring Blacks
                from the American Revolutionary Army. Oct. 13.
                Lord Dunmore, royal governor of Virginia, issued a proc-
                lamation offering freedom to all male slaves who joined the
                British forces. Nov. 7.
                General George Washington, alarmed by the response to
                Dunmore's Proclamation, ordered recruiting officers to ac-
                cept free Blacks. December 31.

Thomas Paine wrote his first published essay in the cause of abolition in a Pennsylvania newspaper.
The first lodge of Negro Free Masons was founded by Prince Hall. July 3.

1776   Continental Congress approved Washington's action of permitting free Blacks to enlist in the Revolutionary Army. Jan. 16.
Mason-Dixon line named for two English surveyors. Feb. 18.
Phillis Wheatley was invited by General Washington to visit him at his headquarters in Cambridge, Mass., so that he might express appreciation for her poem in his honor. Feb. 28.
The Declaration of Independence was adopted without section denouncing slave trade, one of the original grievances against the British king. July 4.
Two Blacks, Prince Whipple and Oliver Cromwell, were with General Washington on Christmas day when he crossed the Delaware. Dec. 25.
Gabriel Prosser, leader of historic slave revolt in Virginia, born a slave.

1777   Vermont was the first state to abolish slavery. July 2.

1778   Four hundred Blacks held off fifteen hundred British in the Battle of Rhode Island. Aug. 28.
More than three thousand Blacks fought in the Revolutionary War.

1779   Twenty slaves petitioned the New Hampshire legislature to abolish slavery. Nov. 12.
Anthony Wayne's victory at Stony Point made possible by the spying of "Pompey," a Black soldier.

1780   Pennsylvania passed a law for the gradual abolition of slavery.
Lott Carey, an early Negro Baptist missionary, born.
First license to a Black preacher granted.

1783   Revolutionary War soldiers, "The Black Regiment," disbanded at Saratoga, N.Y. June 13.
Treaty of Paris, Article VII, promised return to Americans all Negro slaves.

1784   North Carolina answered petition of Edward Griffin, Black
                Revolutionary soldier, commended his meritorious service,
                and freed him. May 4.
                Phillis Wheatley died in Boston. Dec. 5.

1785   Constitutional Convention approved three clauses protecting
                slavery. Sept. 17.
                David Walker, first Black to attack slavery in published
                writings, born in Wilmington, North Carolina. Sept. 28.

1786   Arthur Tappan, leading white abolitionist, born. May 22.

1787   Congress added a provision to the Northwest Ordinance
                forbidding slavery in the territory covered by the Ordinance.
                July 13.
                First free school in New York City, the African Free School,
                opened. Nov. 1.

1788   Andrew Bryan ordained the first pastor of the First African
                Baptist Church organized in Savannah, Georgia. Jan. 19-20.

1789   Josiah Henson, the model for Harriet Beecher Stowe's "Uncle
                Tom," of the famed novel, was born a slave in Maryland;
                he later became a leading abolitionist orator. June 15.

1790   The Pennsylvania Abolition Society petitioned Congress to
                abolish slavery. Feb. 3.
                Samuel Cornish born in Delaware.
                First United States census showed Black population of
                757,181, with 59,557 free.

1791   Benjamin Banneker was appointed, at the suggestion of
                Thomas Jefferson, to serve as member of commission
                headed by L'enfant to lay out plans for the city of Washing-
                ton in District of Columbia.

1792   Antoine Blanc founded the first Negro Catholic sisterhood
                in the United States. Oct. 11.

1793   Benjamin Lundy, colonizationist, born. Jan. 4.
                First fugitive slave law enacted by Congress, making it
                criminal offense to protect a fugitive slave. Feb. 12.
                Eli Whitney invented cotton gin which influenced mass im-
                portation of Blacks and thereby strengthened slaver as an
                institution.

Dr. Benjamin Rush of Philadelphia sought the aid of the Blacks of the city to administer medicines and care for the sick during yellow fever epidemic. It was believed that Blacks were immune.

1794   Richard Allen organized African Methodist Episcopal Church. June 10.
St. Thomas Church, Philadelphia, first Episcopal Negro Congregation, organized. Oct. 12.

1796   Zion Methodist Church organized in New York City.

1797   First petition by Blacks was submitted to Congress protesting a North Carolina law requiring Blacks who were freed by their Quaker masters to be returned to the state and to their slavery status. The petition was rejected. Jan. 30.
Sojourner Truth, leading abolitionist figure in Black history, born a slave in Hurley, New York.

1798   Thaddeus Koscuisko, Polish patriot, left will providing for education of Blacks. May 5.
James P. Beckwourth, scout for General Fremont and noted pioneer and explorer of the West, born in Virginia.
Levi Coffin, organizer of the underground railroad, born. Oct. 28.

1799   Alexander Pushkin, Russian Black poet, born in Moscow.

1800   The free Blacks of Philadelphia presented a petition to Congress opposing the slave trade, the Fugitive Act of 1793, and the institution of slavery itself. Jan. 2.
Gabriel Prosser, a Virginia slave, was betrayed in his plot to lead thousands of slaves in an attack on Richmond, Virginia. Dozens of slaves were imprisoned or hanged on the spot, and Gabriel himself was publicly hanged. Aug. 30.
John Brown born in Torrington, Connecticut. May 9.
James Derham began practicing medicine in New Orleans.
Nat Turner, destined to lead another major slave rebellion, born a slave in Southhampton County, Virginia. Oct. 2.

1802   Alexander Dumas, French novelist of Black extraction, born in France.

1803   Lunsford Lane, noted lecturer for the American Anti-Slavery Society, born a slave in Raleigh, North Carolina.
Toussaint L'ouverture, slave leader of Haitian Revolution, died. April 27.

1804   The Ohio legislature enacted the first of the "Black Laws"
            which restricted rights and movements of Negroes in the
            North; other Northern states soon passed similar legislation.
            Jan. 5.

1805   Benjamin Banneker died. Oct. 9.
            William E. Dodge, proponent of Black education, born.

1806   Maria Weston Chapman, abolitionist, born. July 25.
            Norbert Rillieux, inventor and scientist, born in New Or-
            leans.

1807   British Parliament abolished the slave trade. March 25.
            Ira F. Aldridge, one of the greatest Shakespearean actors
            of his time, was born in New York City.
            Charles Bennet Ray, minister, editor, lecturer, organizer,
            and abolitionist, born in Massachusetts.

1808   Federal law barring the African slave trade went into effect.
            Jan. 1.

1809   Abraham Lincoln born in Harden County, Kentucky. Feb.
            12.
            James W. C. Pennington, leader in the Free Negro Conven-
            tion Movement which outlined an ideology and tactics for
            the Black protest in the 19th century, born a slave in Wash-
            ington County, Maryland.
            Abyssinian Baptist Church organized in New York City.
            July 5.

1810 February Charles Lenox Remond, leader of the American Anti-Slavery
            Society, born in Massachusetts. Feb. 1.
            Thomy Lafon, philanthropist who supported the American
            Anti-Slavery society and the underground railroad, born in
            New Orleans.
      August Theodore Parker, liberal minister, born. Aug. 24.
     October Cassius M. Clay, Kentucky emancipationist, born. Oct. 19.
            David Ruggles, founder of Mirror of Liberty--first Black
            periodical--born.

1811 January Charles Sumner, great New England advocate of Black rights,
            born. Jan. 6.
      February Rev. Daniel A. Payne, African Methodist Episcopalian, who
            established Union Seminary near Columbus, Ohio, born.
            Feb. 24.
         June Harriet Beecher Stowe, author of Uncle Tom's Cabin, born.
            June 14.

1812   Martin R. Delaney, newspaper editor and author, Union
                Army Major, born. May 6.
                George Washington, pioneer, humanitarian and founder of
                Centralia, Washington, born a slave. Aug. 15.
                The Union Church of Africans, organized and incorporated.
                Sept. 25.
                Bishop Richard Allen and Reverend Absalom Jones were re-
                quested to help organize defenses for Philadelphia against
                the British who had recently attacked Washington.
                John Johnson, one of many Blacks who served in the Navy on
                the Great Lakes during the War of 1812, was described by
                his commander after his death in a naval battle: "When
                America has such tars, she has little to fear from tyrants
                of the ocean."

1813   Henry Ward Beecher, promoter for equal rights, born.
                June 24.
                James McCune Smith born of slaves in New York City.

1814   Daniel Reaves Goodloe, North Carolinan emancipationist,
                born. May 28.
                General Andrew Jackson appealed to free Blacks to fight as
                part of the militia. Sept. 21.
                New York legislature authorized the raising of two Black
                regiments. As a result 2000 Blacks were enlisted and sent
                to the army at Sacketts Harbor. Oct. 24.

1815   Henry Highland Garnet, minister, abolitionist, and diplo-
                mat, born a slave in Kent County, Maryland. Dec. 23.
                Myrtilla Miner, founder of Miner's Teachers College, born.
                March 4.

1816   The African Methodist Episcopal Church became independent
                of jurisdictional control by higher all-white bodies. April 9.
                Peter Salem, hero of Bunker Hill, died. Aug. 16.
                John Jones, "the most prominent citizen of Chicago" during
                his lifetime, born in Greene County, North Carolina.
                The Seminole Wars led by General Andrew Jackson began
                with an attack on a fort in western Florida which contained
                hundreds of runaway slaves living among the Creek and
                Seminole Indians who occupied it.
                Bishop Daniel Wayne, reformer and educator, born.

1817   Free Blacks in the large cities held protest meetings against
                the American Colonization Society's efforts to "exile us
                from the land of our nativity." Jan.

Frederick Douglass, orator, editor and statesman, was born a slave in Talbot County, Maryland. Feb. 14.

Victor Sejour, Black Creole poet and dramatist, born. June 2.

The American Colonization Society was organized under the leadership of John C. Calhoun and Henry Clay. Its purpose was to transport free Negroes to Africa. Dec. 28.

Samuel Ringgold Ward, the "Black Daniel Webster," was born in Maryland; he was one of the most noted Black abolitionists. Oct. 17.

James Forten, Black abolitionist, was chairman of the First Negro Convention held in Philadelphia. Jan. 23.

Paul Cuffee, Black shipbuilder and African colonizer, died.

1818   Philadelphia free Blacks established the Pennsylvania Augustine Society, "for the education of people of colour."

St. Philip's Episcopal Church was opened for Blacks in New York City.

Absolom Jones died. Feb. 13.

Charles L. Reason, Black writer, born. July 21.

1820   Missouri Compromise enacted; prohibited slavery north of Missouri. March 3.

Harriet Tubman born a slave in Dorchester County, Maryland.

The American Colonization Society founded Liberia, a Negro Republic in West Africa.

1821   Lott Carey, minister and pioneer leader in Liberia, sailed for that country. Jan. 23.

African Methodist Episcopal Zion Church founded in New York City. June 21.

William Still, author of Underground Railroad and leading underground spokesman, born in New Jersey. Oct. 7.

Alexander Crummell, one of the most highly educated Blacks of his time, born.

1822   Denmark Vesey planned one of the most extensive slave revolts ever recorded. The plot was betrayed and Vesey together with thirty-six others were executed. July 2.

Hiram R. Revels, first Black United States Senator, was born free in Fayetteville, North Carolina. Sept. 27.

Rev. John Gloucester, first Black minister of a Presbyterian church, died.

1823   Thomas Wentworth Higginson, white commander of Black
            soldiers, born.

1825   Frances Ellen Watkins Harper, poet and orator, born in
            Baltimore, Maryland.

1826   James Madison Bell, poet and abolitionist, born free at Gal-
            lipolis, Ohio. April 3.
            John Russworm was the first Black to graduate from an Amer-
            ican college when he received his degree from Bowdoin Col-
            lege, Maine.
            Ira F. Aldridge made his London debut in Othello; he never
            returned to America and became the most famous Shakes-
            pearean actor of his time on the continent.

1827   Slavery was officially abolished in New York State. July 4.
            Freedom's Journal, the first Black newspaper, was pub-
            lished in New York City by John Russworm and Samuel
            Cornish. March 16.

1828   Lott Carey, first missionary to Liberia, died. April 1.

1829   Walker's Appeal, militant anti-slavery pamphlet published
            by David Walker, was distributed throughout the country
            and aroused the Blacks and provoked slave-holders. Jan.
            18.
            John Mercer Langston born. Dec. 14.

1830   James Augustine Healy, the first Black Roman Catholic bish-
            op in America, born to an Irish planter and a Negro slave
            on a plantation near Macon, Georgia. April 6.
            S. R. Lowry, religious educator, born. Dec. 9.
            United States Bureau of the Census reported 3,777 Black
            heads of families who owned slaves; most of these Blacks
            lived in Louisiana, Maryland, Virginia, North Carolina,
            South Carolina, and Virginia.
            Dan Rice, famous white "blackface" minstrel began per-
            forming "Jump Jim Crow" song-dance--from which song
            the words "Jim Crow" came to be applied to legal segrega-
            tion.

1831   The first issue of the Liberator was published by William
            Lloyd Garrison. Jan. 1.
            Nat Turner led the greatest slave rebellion in the United
            States in Virginia; the whole South was thrown into panic
            and more than one hundred and sixty whites and Negroes
            were killed before the revolt ended. Aug. 21-23.

Bishop John Walden, advocate of Black education, born.
Feb. 11.
Nat Turner executed. Nov. 11.

1832   Joseph P. Rainey, Black Congressman from South Carolina,
born. June 21.
Dr. Edward W. Blyden, distinguished scholar and diplomat,
president of Liberia College, born. Aug. 3.
The New England Anti-Slavery Society was established by
twelve whites at the African Baptist Church in Boston.

1833   Oberlin College opened and admitted Blacks at the outset.
Frederick Douglass escaped from his master and fled to
New York.
The Philadelphia Negro Library was organized.
Henry Macneil Turner, a bishop of the African Methodist
Church and colonizationist, was free-born in Abbeville,
South Carolina.
The American Anti-Slavery Society was organized in Phil-
adelphia by Negro and white abolitionists. Dec. 4.

1834   Slavery abolished in the British Empire. Aug. 1.
Henry Blair was the first Black to receive a patent for an
invention, a corn harvester. Oct. 14.
South Carolina enacted a law prohibiting the teaching of free
or slave Black children.
Black youth leaders formed the Garrison Literary and Bene-
volent Association of New York in order "to begin, in early
life, to assist each other to alleviate the afflicted. . ."
The first school for Blacks in Cincinnati, paid for by them-
selves, was opened.
Bishop Isaac Lane, founder of Lane College in Jackson,
Tennessee, born.
Anti-abolition riot broke out in Philadelphia and continued
for three days and nights.

1835   Fifth National Negro Convention resolved to recommend
that Blacks remove the word "African" from the names of
their institutions and organizations, and also to abandon the
use of the word "colored" when referring to themselves.
June 1-5.
John Greenleaf Whittier published his poem, "My Countrymen in Chains."
New York City Blacks formed a bigilance committee to prevent kidnapping of Blacks and to assist fugitive slaves.
William Whipper helped to found the American Moral Reform Society, a Black abolitionist group.

1836   Theodore S. Wright, first Black to receive a degree from a
            theological seminary in the United States (Princeton). Nov. 5.

1837   P. S. B. Pinchback, Black Reconstructionist statesman in
            Louisiana, born. May 10.
            Robert Gould Shaw, Colonel of the 54th Massachusetts Union
            Regiment, first Black company sent from the free states,
            born in Boston of a "proper" Bostonian family which was
            deeply committed to the cause of Black freedom. Oct. 10.
            Elijah P. Lovejoy was murdered by a mob in Alton, Illinois,
            when he refused to stop publishing anti-slavery material.
            Nov. 7.
            James M. Smith, University of Glasgow graduate, conducted
            pioneer work in the scientific study of race.
            William Whipper published "An Address on Non-Resistance
            to Offensive Aggression"--an article written twelve years
            before Thoreau's famous essay on non-violence, and more
            than 125 years before the career of Martin Luther King, Jr.

1838   The first Black periodical, Mirror of Freedom, began pub-
            lishing in New York City. Aug. 30.
            Frederick Douglass escaped from slavery in Baltimore.
            Sept. 3.
            Charles Lenox Remond became first Black lecturer em-
            ployed by an anti-slavery society.

1839   Robert Smalls, Civil War hero and Reconstructionist Con-
            gressman, born in Beaufort, South Carolina. April 5.
            Lunsford Lane of North Carolina made the only abolition
            speech before a southern audience. April 30.
            Benjamin Lundy died. Aug. 22.
            Liberty Party, first anti-slavery political party, organized.
            Nov. 13.
            Whites burned the Black section of Pittsburgh.
            The most famous slave revolt aboard a slave ship took place
            on the Spanish slaver the Amistad. John Quincy Adams, at
            the age of 73 and out of law practice more than thirty years,
            argued the case before the United States Supreme Court.
            Cinque, the young African leader, and his fellow crewmen
            were freed by the Court.

1840   James M. Turner, a Lincoln University founder, born in
            Jefferson City, Missouri. May 16.

1841   Blanche Kelso Bruce, only Black to serve full term in United
            States Senate, born a slave at Prince Edward County, Vir-
            ginia. March 1.

President Tyler sent a message to Congress dealing with
the suppression of the slave trade. June 1.
Frederick Douglass became lecturer for the Massachusetts
Anti-Slavery Society. Aug.
James M. Townsend, first Black to se ve as member of Indiana Legislature, born. Aug. 18.
Slave trader "Creole" was scene of slave revolt. Slaves
took over ship and sailed to Bahamas where they were given
asylum and freedom. Nov.

1842   Robert Brown Elliott, Reconstruction Congressman from
South Carolina, born. Aug. 11.
Charlie Smith, last known slave brought to America, born
in Liberia.
James Forten died in Philadelphia.
Capture of George Latimore in Boston precipitated the first
of several famous fugitive slave cases which embittered
North and South. Boston abolitionists raised enough money
to purchase Latimore from his master. Nov. 17.

1843   Sojourner Truth, first Black woman to become lecturer
against slavery, left New York and began her work as an
abolitionist. June 1.
Henry Highland Garnet made controversial speech at the
National Convention of Colored Men in Buffalo calling for
a slave revolt and a general strike. Aug. 22.
Blacks participated in a national political gathering for the
first time at a meeting of the Liberty Party convention in
Buffalo, New York. Aug. 30.

1844   James Beckwourth discovered a pass through the coast range
to the Pacific Ocean which was named for him, Beckwourth
Pass. April 26.
Elijah J. McCoy, inventor (lubricating cup), born. May 2.
Charles Nash, Congressman from Louisiana, born. May 23.

1845   Macon B. Allen was the first Black formally admitted to the
bar when he passed the examination at Worcester, Massachusetts. May 3.
Narrative of Frederick Douglass published.
Publication of Les Cenelles, in French and English, an
anthology of poetry by Negro poets of New Orleans.
Frederick Douglass delivered the commencement address
at Western Reserve College which was one of the first
Black attempts to refute racism scientifically.

1847   Frederick Douglass began to publish his own newspaper, the
            North Star. Dec. 3.
            William Alexander Leidesdorff, Black businessman, launched
            the first steamboat to sail in San Francisco Bay; he later
            built the first hotel in that city.
            Dred Scott case initiated in St. Louis Circuit Court. June
            30.

1848   Negro blacksmith Lewis Temple invented a Toggle harpoon
            which became the standard harpoon of the American whaling
            industry.
            William and Ellen Craft escaped from slavery in Georgia in
            one of the most dramatic escapes of the period. Dec. 26.

1849   Harriet Tubman escaped from slavery in Maryland. July.
            Archibald H. Grimke, Harvard Law School graduate and
            author of biographies of Charles Sumner and William Lloyd
            Garrison, born near Charleston, South Carolina. Aug. 17.
            Benjamin Roberts filed the first school integration suit on
            behalf of his daughter who had been denied admission to the
            white schools in Boston. The Supreme Court of Massachu-
            setts rejected the suit and established the "separate but
            equal" doctrine.
            "Blind Tom," the greatest musical prodigy of his time,
            born a slave in Georgia.

1850   Fugitive Slave Law passed by Congress as part of the Com-
            promise of 1850; it offered federal officers a fee for cap-
            tured slaves. Sept. 18.

1851   William C. Nell published Services of Colored Americans
            in the Wars of 1776 and 1812, the first full-length study of
            the American Black.
            Walter H. Brooks, distinguished clergyman, born. Aug. 30.

1852   First edition of Uncle Tom's Cabin published. March 20.
            Napoleon issued a decree against the slave trade. March
            29.

1853   First Black YMCA established in Washington, D.C. Jan. 3.
            William Wells Brown wrote Clotel, the first novel by a Black
            American.
            Publication of Solomon Northrup's Narrative of a Slave, one
            of the most famous of the many narratives written by fugi-
            tive slaves telling their stores.

1854   Lincoln University, the first Black college, was chartered
            as Ashmond Institute in Chester, Pennsylvania. Jan. 1.
            August Tolon, first Black Catholic priest to serve in the
            United States, was born in Battle Creek, Missouri. April 1.
            Lucey C. Laney, founder of Haines Institute in Augusta,
            Georgia, born. April 13.
            Kansas-Nebraska Act repealed the Missouri Compromise
            and opened Northern territory to slavery. May 30.
            Anthony Burns was returned to slavery in Virginia in spite
            of an attempt by Boston citizens to purchase his freedom for
            $1200. June 3.
            The Republican Party was created by Free Soilers and Whigs
            as well as Democrats who were opposed to the extension of
            slavery.

1855   Black troops mustered into Confederate service. March 24.

1856   Booker T. Washington born a slave in Franklin County,
            Virginia. April 5.
            Granville T. Woods, inventor of industrial appliances, born.
            April 23.
            Wilberforce University founded by Methodist Episcopal
            Church. Aug. 30

1857   Dred Scott decision by the United States Supreme Court
            opened federal territory to slavery and denied citzenship to
            Black Americans. May 6.
            Dred Scott and his family were freed by the new owner,
            Taylor Blow. May 26.

1858   Daniel Hale Williams, called the "Father of Negro Hospitals,"
            born in Hollidayburg, Pennsylvania. Jan. 18.
            Twelve whites and thirty-four Negroes attended John Brown's
            anti-slavery convention in Chatham, Canada. May 8.
            Charles W. Chestnutt, Black pioneer novelist, born. June
            20.
            Lecompton, Kansas constitution, sanctioning slavery, re-
            jected. Aug. 2.
            William Wells Brown published The Escape, first play writ-
            ten by an American Black.

1859   Henry O. Tanner, world famous artist, born in Pittsburgh.
            June 21.
            John Brown met for last time with Frederick Douglass at
            an old quarry in Chambersburg, Pennsylvania. Aug. 19.
            John Brown raided Harper's Ferry. Oct. 16.

The last slave ship, <u>Clothilde</u>, landed its cargo of slaves at Mobile, Alabama.

Samuel Cornish, one of the first men to approach the race problem from an economic point of view, died.

John Brown hanged at Charles Town, West Virginia. Dec. 2.

1860   George Washington Carver born in Diamond Grove, Missouri.

Abraham Lincoln elected President. Nov. 6.

South Carolina declared herself an "independent commonwealth." Dec. 18.

1861   Robert Smalls (Union Navy pilot) watching preparations for the attack on Fort Sumter, said "this, boys, is the dawn of freedom for our race." April 10.

Confederates attacked Fort Sumter. April 12.

Lincoln issued proclamation calling for 75,000 volunteers from the states. April 15.

Loyal Black volunteers were not accepted when the first call for troops was made.

Clara Barton with five Black girls gave aid to the wounded in the passage through Baltimore. April 21.

General B. F. Butler refused to return three escaped slaves as they were "contraband of war." May 24.

General George B. McClellan, Ohio Department, issued orders to suppress any Black attempts at insurrection. May 26.

Black Mass Meeting offered to raise an army of 50,000 men and that the women would serve as nurses, etc. May 31.

Hampton Institute's first day, with Mary S. Peake, as the first Black teacher. Aug. 17.

The Secretary of the Navy authorized the enlistment of Black slaves later in the year. Sept. 25.

1862   President Lincoln recommended to Congress gradual, compensated emancipation. March 6.

United States Senate passed bill abolishing slavery in the District of Columbia. April 4.

Robert Smalls, Black pilot, sailed armed Confederate steamer, the <u>Planter</u>, out of Charleston, South Carolina, and presented her to the United States Navy. May 13.

Liberia recognized as a free nation by the United States. June 3.

Lincoln recommended aid to states abolishing slavery. July 14.

The first regular colored troops were enlisted at Leaven-
worth, Kansas. July 17.
Anthony Burns, Baptist clergyman whose capture as a fugi-
tive slave caused a riot in Boston, died. July 27.
Charlotte Forten, Black poet and teacher, arrived in St.
Helena, South Carolina, to teach Blacks. Oct. 29.
First African Methodist Episcopal Church established at
New Bern, North Carolian. Dec. 27.

1863   President Lincoln signed the Emancipation Proclamation.
Jan. 1.
The War Department authorized Massachusetts governor to
recruit Black troops. The Fifty-fourth Massachusetts Vol-
unteers was the first Black regiment raised in the North.
Jan. 26.
Two Black infantry regiments, First and Second, South
Carolina, captured and occupied Jacksonville, Florida,
causing panic along the Southern seabord. March 10.
Confederate Congress passed resolution which branded
Black troops and their officers criminals; thus caputred
Black soldiers could be put to death or slavery. May 1.
Eight Black regiments played important role in the seige
of Port Hudson which, with the fall of Vicksburg, gave the
Union control of the Mississippi River and cut the Confed-
eracy into two sections. July 9.
The New York City Draft Riots were the bloodiest in Amer-
ican history. July 13-17.
The Fifty-fourth Massachusetts Volunteers made a charge
on Fort Wagner in Charleston Harbor, South Carolina. At
least one member of the all-Black regiment won the Con-
gressional Medal of Honor for his bravery. July 18.
Kelly Miller, author and educator, born. July 18.
Dr. Mary Church Terrell, first president of the National
Association of Colored Women, born. Sept. 23.

1864   Famous Battle of Fort Pillow and the massacre of Black
troops after its surrender. April 12.
In a duel between USS Kearsage and CSS Alabama off the
coast of France, a Black sailor, Joachim Pease, displayed
"marked coolness," and won the Congressional Medal of
Honor. June 19.
Fugitive slave laws repealed. June 28.
Maryland constitution amended to abolish slavery. July 7.
Although he himself was not certain of actual date, George
Washington Carver celebrated his birthday on this date.
July 12.

New Orleans Tribune began publishing as the first daily
Black newspaper in French and English. Oct. 14.
Richard B. Harrison, featured actor who created the role of
"De Lawd" in Green Pastures, born. Aug. 28.
Congress passed a bill equalizing for the first time the pay,
arms, equipment and medical services of Black troops.
Charles Young (Colonel), West Point graduate who held the
highest rank in his time, born.
"Blind Boone," John W. Boone, a noted musical prodigy,
born in Miami, Missouri.
First public school system for Blacks opened in the District
of Columbia.

1865 General Lee said that it was "not only expedient but neces-
sary" that the Confederate Army use Black slaves as soldiers.
Jan. 11.
John S. Rock was the first Black to practice before the United
States Supreme Court. Feb. 1.
Henry Highland Garnet was the first Black to preach in the
Capitol delivering a sermon on the abolition of slavery.
Feb. 12.
Congress passed a bill giving freedom to wives and children
of Black soldiers. March 3.
The Freedman's Bureau established by Congress to help the
newly emancipated slaves. March 13.
Abraham Lincoln died from wounds received when shot at
Ford's Theater by actor John Wilkes Booth. April 15.
Two white regiments and a Negro regiment, the 62nd USCT,
fought the last action of the Civil War at White's Ranch,
Texas. Sergeant Crocket, a Black, believed to have been the
last man to shed blood in the War. May 13.
President Andrew Johnson announced his Reconstruction
plan. May 29.
South Carolina abolished slavery. Aug. 27.
Timothy T. Fortune, journalist and founder of the New York
Age, born. Oct. 3.
Congress passed the Thirteenth Amendment which, on rati-
fication, abolished slavery in the United States. Dec. 18.
Fisk University opened. April 20.
Patrick Henry Healy was the first Black to win the Doctor
of Philosophy degree when he passed his final examination
in Louvain, Belgium. July 26.
Matthew A. Henson, Black explorer who accompanied Peary
to the North Pole, born in Charles County, Maryland. Aug-
ust 8.

Edward G. Walker and Charles L. Mitchell were elected
to the Massachusetts House of Representatives thus becoming the first Blacks elected to an American legislative assembly.
Ku Klux Klan organized in Tennessee.
Shaw University founded.
Howard University founded as Howard Seminary in Washington, D.C. Nov. 20.

1867   Talladega and Morehouse College opened. Feb.
Peabody Educational Fund established for the South. Feb. 7.
Maggie Lena Walker, the first woman bank president in
the United States, born in Richmond, Virginia.
Robert R. Moton, outstanding educator, born. Aug. 26.
William Still led a successful campaign against segregated
streetcars in Philadelphia.
Samuel Ringgold Ward died in the British West Indies.

1868   William Edward Burghardt Du Bois born in Great Barrington,
Massachusetts. Feb. 23.
Hampton Institute opened. April
Fourteenth Amendment became part of the Constitution.
July 28.
John Hope, educator, born. June 2.
Oscar J. Dunn, ex-slave, became Lieutenant Governor of
Louisiana, the highest elective office then held by a Black
American. June 13.

1869   Will Marion Cook, famed composer, born. Jan. 27.
Jefferson P. Long from Georgia was seated as the first
Negro in the House of Representatives.
The American Anti-Slavery Society was dissolved.
Ebenezer Don Carlos Bennett was the first Black to receive
an appointment in the diplomatic service when he became
Minister to Haiti. April 16.

1870   Fifteenth Amendment adopted, giving the Black the right to
vote. March 30.
Thomas Peterson was the first Black to vote in the United
States the day after the Fifteenth Amendment was ratified.
Robert S. Abbott, founder of the Chicago Defender, born
on St. Simon's Island off the coast of Georgia. Nov. 24.
James W. C. Pennington died.
Freedman's Bureau expired by law.

1871   James Weldon Johnson, poet, educator, civil rights fighter,
        first Black consul to Nicaragua, born in Jacksonville, Flor-
        ida. June 17.
        Fisk Jubilee Singers made their first appearances under the
        direction of George L. White.
        Oscar De Priest, first Black Congressman elected from a
        northern state (Illinois), born.

1872   Booker T. Washington entered Hampton Institute.
        Paul Laurence Dunbar, nationally-known poet and short story
        writer, born in Dayton, Ohio. June 27.
        John H. Conyers was the first Black admitted to the United
        States Naval Academy. Oct. 21.
        P.B.S. Pinchback became Acting Governor of Louisiana on
        the impeachment of the Governor. Dec. 11.
        First Black police officer appointed in Chicago.
        Charlotte E. Ray, the first Black woman lawyer, graduated
        from Howard University Law School; she was first woman
        to graduate from a university law school.
        William Still published the records of the fugitive slaves in
        the classic, Underground Railroad.

1873   Slavery abolished in Puerto Rico. March 23.
        John W. Work, musician, Black folk singer expert, born.
        Aug. 6.
        W. C. Handy, "Father of the Blues," born in Florence,
        Alabama. Nov. 16.
        Richard T. Greener, first Black graduate of Harvard Uni-
        versity, named professor of metaphysics at the University
        of South Carolina.

1874   William C. Nell died. May 25.
        Patrick Henry Healy, Black inaugurated as President of
        Georgetown University, oldest Catholic university in the
        United States. July 31.

1875   Blacks massacred at Hamburg, South Carolina. July 9.
        Civil Rights Bill enacted by Congress contained equal ac-
        commodations provisions. March 1.
        Mary McLeod Bethune, noted educator, born in Mayesville,
        South Carolina. July 10.
        Blanche K. Bruce became a member of the United States
        Senate from Mississippi, the only Black to serve a full
        term in the Senate. March 15.
        Carter G. Woodson, scholar and historian, born in New
        Canton, Virginia. Dec. 19.
        Booker T. Washington graduated from Hampton Institute.

1876   E. M. Bannister, Black painter, exhibited and received
            first prize for his "under the Oaks" at the Philadelphia
            Centennial Exposition. July 4.
            Edward A. Bounchet received the Doctor of Philosophy de-
            gree in physics at Yale University, the first Black awarded
            the doctorate by an American university.
            "Bert" Williams, described by Billboard as "the greatest
            comedian on the American stage" in the early 1900's, born
            in the Bahamas.

1877   Meta Vaux Fuller, noted sculptress of the 19th Century, born
            June 9.
            Henry O. Flipper, born a slave in Georgia, was the first
            Black graduate from West Point. June 15.
            Frederick Doublass appointed Marshal of the District of
            Columbia by President Rutherford B. Hayes.
            Reconstruction ended with the withdrawal of all Union troops
            from the South.

1879   William Lloyd Garrison died. May 24.
            Blanche K. Bruce presided over the United States Senate.
            Feb. 15.

1871   William Ickins, orator, author and equal rights fighter,
            born. Jan 15.
            Frederick Douglass appointed Recorder of Deeds for the
            District of Columbia. May 17.
            Booker T. Washington began his work at Tuskegee Institute.
            July 4.

1882   Mrs. Violette A. Johnson, first Black woman admitted to
            practice before the United States Supreme Court, born.
            July 16.
            Benjamin Brawley, social historian, born. April 22.
            Charlotte Hawkins Brown, founder of the Palmer Institute
            at Sedalia, North Carolina, born.
            John F. Slater Fund of one million dollars was created for
            education and uplifting the Blacks in the South.
            Robert Morris, first Black to practice in the courts of the
            United States, died. Dec. 11.
            First Jim Crow railroad car law passed in Tennessee--be-
            ginning of modern segregation movement as other Southern
            states followed.

1883   Shoe lasting machine patented by Jan Matzeliger, American
            Black inventor. March 20.

Spellman College organized in basement of church in Atlanta, Goergia. April 11.

Ernest Everett Just, biologist known for research in marine eggs, born. Aug. 14.

Sojourner Truth died in Battle Creek, Michigan. Nov. 26.

George Washington Williams wrote a History of the Negro Race in America, the first serious history undertaken by a Negro.

1884   The Medico-Chirugical Society of the District of Columbia, oldest Black American medical society, organized. April 24.

John Roy Lynch, former Congressman, was elected temporary chairman of the Republican convention, the first Black to preside over deliberations of a national political party. June 3.

Robert Brown Elliott, Reconstructionist, died. Aug. 9.

William Wells Brown died in Cambridge, Massachusetts.

1886   The first electric trolly on the American continent was run by a Black, L. Clark Brooks. May 24.

George Washington Cable published a frank treatment of Negro problems in The Silent South.

William Whipper, underground railroad leader, died.

1888   Slavery in Brazil abolished. May 14.

1889   Provident Hospital was incorporated in Chicago with the first training school for Black nurses. Jan. 23.

Asa Philip Randolph, labor leader, born in Crescent City, Florida. April 15.

Frederick Douglass appointed United States Minister to Haiti.

1891   Peter Jackson, great Black boxer, fought sixty-one round draw with James J. Corbett. May 21.

1892   Luther P. Jackson, Black historian, born in Lexington, Kentucky. July 11.

Lynchings in the United States reached their peak.

1893   Walter Francis White, long-time Executive Secretary of the NAACP, born in Atlanta, Georgia. July 1.

Dr. Daniel Hale Williams performed the world's first successful heart operation at Chicago's Provident Hospital. July 9.

1895   Frederick Douglass died in Anacosta Heights, District of
               Columbia, where his home is now a national shrine. Feb.
               20.
               Booker T. Washington delivered his famous "Atlanta Com-
               promise" address at Cotton Exposition in Atlanta, Georgia.
               Sept. 18.
               William Grant Still, orchestral musician and composer ("Afro-
               American Symphony") born. May 11.
               Charles E. Houston, considered one of the great constitu-
               tional lawyers in American history, born.
               W. E. B. Du Bois received his doctorate degree from Har-
               vard University, the first Black to receive this degree from
               Harvard. June.
               Ida B. Well compiled the first statistical pamphlet on lynch-
               ing, The Red Record.

1896   United States Supreme Court decision of Plessy v. Ferguson
               upheld doctrine of "separate but equal." May 18.
               National Association of Colored Women organized in Wash-
               ington, D.C. by Dr. Mary Church Terrell. July 21.
               W. E. B. Du Bois' The Suppression of the African Slave
               Trade was published as the first volume in the Harvard His-
               torical Studies Series.
               Booker T. Washington received the first honorary degree
               awarded to a Black by Harvard University.

1897   H. A. Rucker served as Collector of Internal Revenue in
               Georgia. Nov. 4.
               John Mercer Langston of Virginia, soldier, educator, Hai-
               tian consul, Congressman, died. Nov. 15.

1898   Blanche K. Bruce died in Washington, D.C. March 17.
               Bob Cole's A Trip to Coontown was the first musical comedy
               written by a Black for Black talent.
               The North Carolina Mutual Life Insurance Company was or-
               ganized by John Merrick and Dr. A. M. Moore in Durham,
               North Carolina.

1899   Edward Kennedy ("Duke") Ellington born in Washington,
               D.C. April 4.

1900   Louis Armstrong born in New Orleans. July 4.
               James Augustine Healy died in Portland, Maine. Aug. 5.
               Charles W. Chestnutt published his first novel, The House
               Behind the Cedars.

1901   Hiram R. Revels died in Holy Springs, Mississippi. Jan.
            16.
            William M. Trotter founded the Boston Guardian, a militant
            newspaper which advocated absolute equality for Blacks.

1903   Countee Cullen, distinguished Black poet of the twenties,
            born. May 30.
            W. E. B. Du Bois published his Souls of Black Folk.

1904   Dr. Charles R. Drew, "Father of Blood Plasma," born.
            June 3.
            Dr. Ralph J. Bunche born in Washington, D.C. Aug. 7.

1905   Group of Black intellectuals organized the so-called Niagra
            Movement at a meeting near Niagra Falls. July 11-13.
            Robert S. Abbott began publication of the Chicago Defender,
            the most influential and militant Black newspaper.

1906   Paul Laurence Dunbar the poet died in Dayton, Ohio. Feb. 9.
            The Atlanta race riot resulted in the death of twelve people.
            Sept. 22.
            Alpha Phi Alpha, the first Black Greek letter society was
            organized as a fraternity. Dec. 4.

1907   Alaine L. Locke of Harvard was the first Black American
            Rhodes Scholar.
            Jack Johnson defeated Tommy Burns for the heavy-weight
            championship at Sydney, Australia.

1908   Thurgood Marshall born in Baltimore, Maryland. Nov. 29.

1909   NAACP founded on Lincoln's birthday after a savage Spring-
            field, Illinois, lynching. Feb. 12.
            Commander Robert E. Perry reached the North Pole accom-
            panied by his "Negro assistant," Matthew H. Henson. April
            6.
            Miss Caroline Phelp-Stokes of New York, who created a fund
            for the education of Blacks, died.
            Nannie Burroughs founded the National Training School for
            Women at Washington, D.C.

1910   W. E. B. Du Bois started Crisis as the official organ of the
            NAACP.
            National Urban League organized in New York City. April.

1912   W. C. Handy published the first blues composition, Mem-
            phis Blues. Sept. 27.

1913   Harriet Tubman died in Auburn, New York. March 10.

1914   Joe Louis (Barrow) born in Lexington, Alabama. May 13.
                The Spingarn Medal awards were instituted by Joel E. Spin-
                garn, Chairman of the Board of Directors of the NAACP, to
                call to the attention of the American people the existence of
                distinguished merit and achievement among colored Amer-
                icans.

1915   Professor Ernest E. Just received the first Spingarn Medal
                for researches in the field of biology. Feb. 12.
                Guinn v. United States declared "grandfather clauses" in
                the Maryland and Oklahoma constitutions null and void.
                June 21.
                Association of the Study of Negro Life and History founded
                by Dr. Carter G. Woodson. Sept. 9.
                Booker T. Washington died in Tuskegee, Alabama. Nov. 14.
                Private Stephen Little, Co. O. 12th Infantry, killed in action,
                Nogales, Arizona; military camp named in his honor. Nov.
                26.
                Dr. Robert Russa Moton elected principal, Tuskegee Nor-
                mal and Industrial Institute. Dec. 20.
                About 2,000,000 Southern Blacks moved to Northern indus-
                trial centers after the "great migration" began in this year.

1916   Major Charles Young received Spingarn Medal for services
                in Liberia. Feb. 22.

1917   United States entered World War I.
                Harry T. Burleigh, composer, pianist, singer, awarded
                Spingarn Medal for excellence in the field of creative music.
                May 16.
                Julius Rosenwald Fund for Education, Scientific and Reli-
                gious Purposes was organized. Oct. 30.
                Six hundred Blacks were commissioned officers during
                World War I.
                Edward A. Johnson first Black to be elected to the New York
                State Assembly. Nov. 23.
                Emmett J. Scott was appointed special assistant to the Sec-
                retary of War.

1918   William Stanley Braithwaite, poet, literary critic and edi-
                tor, received Spingarn medal for distinguished achievement
                in literature. May 5.
                National Liberty Congress of Colored Americans petitioned
                Congress to make lynching a federal crime. July 29.

First soldiers in American army to be decorated for bravery in France were two Blacks, Henry Johnson and Needham R Roberts.

1919   First Pan African Congress, organized by W. E. B. Du Bois, met at Grand Hotel in Paris. Feb. 19-21.
Archibald K. Grimke, former U.S. Consul in Santo Domingo, author and president of the NAACP branch in the District of Columbia for seventy years, received the Spingarn Medal for distinguished service to his race and country. June 27.
There were eighty-three lynchings, the KKK held more than two hundred public meetings across the country, and there were twenty-five major race riots in the country this year.

1920   W. E. B. Du Bois awarded Spingarn Medal for his achieve-ments in scholarship, as editor of Crisis, and for founding and calling of the Pan African Congress. June 1.
National Convention of Marcus Garvey's Universal Improve-ment Association opened in Liberty Hall in Harlem; Garvey's black nationalist movement reached its peak during this year. Aug. 1.
Emperor Jones, by O'Neill, opened at the Provincetown Theatre starring Charles Gilpin in the title role. Nov. 3.

1921   Charles S. Gilpin, actor, received the Spingarn Medal for his performance in the title role of Eugene O'Neill's drama, Emperor Jones. June 30.
Marcus Garvey inaugurated provisional president of the "Republic of Africa." Aug. 31.
The doctor of philosophy degree was awarded for the first time to Black women: Evan B. Dykes, English at Radcliffe; Sadie T. Mossell, Economics at the University of Pennsyl-vania; Georgiana R. Simpson, German at the University of Chicago.

1922   Colonel Charles Young died in Liberia. Jan. 7.
Congress passed the Dyer Anti-Lynching Bill. Jan. 26.
Mary B. Talbert, former president of the National Associ-ation of Colored Women, awarded Spingarn Medal for ser-vice to the women of her race and the restoration of the Frederick Douglass home. June 20.
Frederick Douglass Memorial Home in Washington, D.C. dedicated as museum. Aug. 12.

1923   Spingarn Medal awarded to George Washington Carver, head of the Department of Research, and director of the

Experiment Station at Tuskegee Institute, Alabama, for distinguished research in agricultural chemistry. Sept. 4.
First Catholic seminary for the education of Black priests
was dedicated in Bay St. Louis, Mississippi. Sept. 16.
United States Department of Labor estimated that almost
500,000 Blacks left the South during the previous twelve
months. Oct. 24.
Charles S. Johnson began to edit Opportunity: A Journal of
Negro Life for the Urban League.

1924   Roland Hayes, singer, given Spingarn Medal for his great
artistry through which he "so finely interpreted the beauty
and charm of the Negro folk song" and won for himself a
place as soloist with the Boston Symphony Orchestra. July 1.
Fletcher Henderson, first musician to make name with
jazz band, opened at Roseland Ballroom on Broadway. Oct. 3.

1925   Charles Drew of Washington, D.C. won Amherst College
Ashley Grid Trophy for being most valuable member of the
1924 squad. Jan. 1.
Adelbert H. Roberts elected to Illinois state legislature--
first Negro since reconstruction days. Jan. 10.
Greewood, Mississippi, ministers and prominent business-
men led mob which lynched two Blacks. March 14.
Countee P. Cullen, New York University poet, awarded
honorary Phi Beta Kappa key. March 28.
Mob at Oscella, Louisiana, flogged and shot minister for
"preaching equality." April 18.
A. Philip Randolph organized Brotherhood of Sleeping Car
Porters, a labor union. May 8.
Harry T. Burleigh honored by Temple Emmanuel Congregation of New York City at end of 25th year as soloist.
May 16.
James Weldon Johnson, former U.S. consul in Venezuela
and Nicaragua, former editor, secretary, NAACP, poet
received Spingarn Medal for distinguished achievements
as author, diplomat and public servant. June 30.
Louis Armstrong recorded first of "Hot Five and Hot Seven"
recordings which influenced jazz. Nov. 11.

1926   Spingarn Medal to Carter G. Woodson, historian and founder
of the Association for the Study of Negro Life and History,
for ten years' devoted service in collecting and publishing
the records of the Black in America. June 29.
Dr. William S. Scarborough, scholar and educator, died.
Aug. 9.

1927 United States Supreme Court struck down law in Texas barring Blacks from voting "white primary." March 7.
Anthony Overton, businessman, given Spingarn Medal for his successful business career climaxed by the admission of his company as the first Black organization permitted to do insurance business under the rigid requirements of the State of New York. June 28.

1928 Charles W. Chestnutt, author, awarded Spingarn Medal for his "pioneer work as a literary artist depicting the life and struggle of Americans of Negro descent, and for his long and useful career as scholar, worker and freeman in one of America's greatest cities." July 3.
Oscar de Priest was the first Black from non-Southern state to be elected to Congress. Nov. 6.

1929 Martin Luther King, Jr. born in Atlanta, Georgia. Jan. 15.
Brotherhood of Sleeping Car Porters received charter from AFL. Feb. 23.
Mordecai Wyatt Johnson, president of Howard University, received Spingarn Medal "for his successful administration as first Black president of the leading Black university in America, and especially for his leadership in securing, during the past year, legal authority for appropriations to Howard University by the government of the United States." July 2.
W. T. Francis, appointed American consul to Liberia by President Coolidge, died in Africa. July 15.
There were ten known lynchings in the United States during the year; Florida led with four.
Francis E. Rivers first Black admitted to the New York Bar Association.

1930 Green Pastures opened on Broadway featuring Richard B. Harrison as "De Lawd." Feb. 26.
Spingarn Medal to Henry A. Hunt, principal for Fort Valley High and Industrial School "for twenty-five years of modest, faithful, unselfish and devoted service in the education of colored people of rural Georgia and the teaching profession in that state." May 3.
The New York Times announced that the "n" in "Negro" would hereafter be capitalized. June 7.
Mrs. Mary McLeod Bethune was selected as one of the fifty leading women of America compiled by contemporary social historian Ida Tarbell. June 22.
Joel E. Spingarn elected President of NAACP.

Charles Gilpin, noted actor, died.
Jack Thompson became welterweight champion of the world
when he defeated Jackie Fields. May 9.

1931   Richard B. Harrison received Spingarn Medal for his "fine
and reverent characterization of the Lord in Marc Connelly's
play, The Green Pastures (which) has made that play the outstanding dramatic accomplishment in the year 1931. But the
Medal is given to Mr. Harrison not simply for this crown-
ing accomplishment, but for the long years of his work as
dramatic reader and entertainer, interpreting to the mass of
colored people in church and school the finest specimens of
English drama from Shakespeare down. It is fitting that in
the sixty-seventh year of his life he should receive widespread acclaim for a role that typifies and completes his life
work." March 22.
The cause celebre trial of the decade, the Scottsboro trial,
began in Alabama. April 6.
Dr. Daniel Hale Williams, founder of Chicago's Provident
Hospital, died. Aug. 4.

1932   Spingarn Medal to Robert Russa Moton, principal of Tuskegee
Institute, "for his thoughtful leadership of conservative opin-
io   ion and action on the Negro in the United States, as shown
in the U.S. Veterans' Hospital controversy at Tuskegee; by
his stand on education in Haiti; by his support of equal opportunity for the Negro in the American public school system; and by his expression of the best ideals of the Negro
in his book, What the Negro Thinks." May 20.

1933   NAACP made its first attack on segregation and discrimination in education and filed suit against the University of
North Carolina on behalf of Thomas Hocutt; case was lost
on technicality. March 15.
Max Yergan, for ten years American Y.M.C.A. secretary
among the native students of South Africa, received the
Spingarn Medal as "a missionary of intelligence, tact and
self-sacrifice, representing the gift of cooperation and culture which American Negroes may send back to their Moth-
erland; and he inaugurated last year an unusual local movement for interracial understanding among black and white
students." July 1.

1934   Mississippi Senate passed a law permitting a private citizen,
one C. W. Collins, to spring the trap to hang three Blacks
accused of raping Collins' daughter. March 10.

Spingarn Medal to William Taylor Buwell Williams, dean of
Tuskegee Institute, "for his long service as field agent of the
Slater and Jeanes Funds and the General Education Board,
his comprehensive knowledge of the field of Negro education
and educational equipment, and his sincere efforts for their
betterment." June 29.
Arthur Mitchell defeated Oscar de Priest for the Illinois
Congressional seat held by the latter. Nov. 7.
Dr. W. E. B. Du Bois resigned as editor of the Crisis.
Bishop W. Sampson Brooks, founder of Monrovia College in
Liberia, died in San Antonio, Texas.

1935   Richard B. Harrison died in New York City. March 18.
Joe Louis defeated Primo Carnera at Yankee Stadium.
June 25.
Spingarn Medal to Mrs. Mary McLeod Bethune, founder and
president of Bethune Cookman College, Daytona Beach, Florida. "In the face of almost insuperable difficulties she has,
almost single-handedly, established and built up Bethune-
Cookman College . . . In doing this she has not simply
created another educational institution. Both the institution's
and Mrs. Bethune's influence have been nationwide. That
influence has always been on a high plane, directed by a
superb courage. Mrs. Bethune has always spoken out
against injustice, in the South as well as in the North, without compromise or fear." June 28.
Maryland Court of Appeals ordered University of Maryland
to admit Donald Mung. Nov. 5.
National Council of Negro Women founded in New York City
with Mrs. Mary McLeod Bethune as president. Dec. 5.

1936   John Hope, president of Atlanta University, winner of the
Spingarn Medal. Characterized by the Committee of Award
as "a distinguished leader of his race, one of the foremost
college presidents in the United States, widely and favorably
known throughout the educational world." July 3.
Jesse Owens won four gold medals at the Berlin Olympics.
Aug. 9.
NAACP filed first suits in campaign to equalize teachers'
salaries and educational facilities. Dec. 8.

1937   William H. Hastie confirmed as judge of Federal District
Court in Virgin Islands, thereby becoming the first Black
federal judge. March 26.
Joe Louis defeated James J. Braddock in Chicago for the
heavyweight boxing championship of the world. June 22.

Walter White, executive secretary of the NAACP, won the
Spingarn Medal for his personal investigation of 41 lynchings
and 8 race riots and for his "remarkable tact, skill and per-
suasiveness" in lobbying for a federal anti-lynching bill.
July 2.
Death of Bessie Smith in Clarksdale, Mississippi. Sept. 26.
Bishop Isaac Lane died at the age of 103.

1938   James Weldon Johnson died. June 24.
First woman Black legislator, Crystal Bird Fauset of Phila-
delphia, elected to the Pennsylvania House of Representatives.
Nov. 8.
United States Supreme Court ruled that states must provide
equal educational facilities within its boundaries. Dec. 12.
No Spingarn Medal awarded this year.

1939   Broadway opening of Mamba's Daughter gave Ethel Waters
her greatest stage triumph. Jan. 14.
D. E. Howard received a patent for his invention of "an
optical apparatus for indicating the position of a tool." Jan.
24.
University of Wisconsin refused gift whose donor limited
use of funds to white students only. Feb. 18.
Mrs. Franklin D. Roosevelt resigned from the organization
of Daughters of Revolution when Marian Anderson was barred
from singing in Constitution Hall in Washington, D.C. March.
Marian Anderson gave her Easter Sunday Open Air recital
in Washington, D.C.
NAACP launched drive to obtain one million signatures on
anti-lynch petition. April 22.
Mississippi Senator Theodore C. Bilbo introduced "Back to
Africa Bill" in the United States Senate. April 23.
Joe Louis knocked out Tony Galento in the 4th round. June 28.
Spingarn Medal to Marian Anderson, contralto, ". . . has
been chosen for her special achievement in the field of
music. Equally with that achievement, which has won her
world-wide fame as one of the greatest singers of our time,
is her magnificent dignity as a human being. Her unassum-
ing manner, which has not been changed by her phenomenal
success, has added to the esteem not only of Marian Anderson as an individual but of the race to which she belongs."
July 2.
J. Matilda Bolin appointed first Black woman judge in the
United States; she was made judge of the Court of Domestic Relations in New York City by Mayor Fiorello La Guardia.
July 22.

NAACP Legal Defense and Educational Fund organized as separate organization. Oct. 11.

1940   Richard Wright's Native Son was published and became one of of the best-sellers of the year. Feb.
Virginia legislature chose "Carry Me Back to Ole Virginia" by Black composer James A. Bland as the state song. April.
Marcus Garvey died in London. June 10.
Louis T. Wright, surgeon, awarded Spingarn Medal "for his contributions to the healing of mankind and for his courageous, uncompromising position held often in the face of bitter attack, that Negro men of medicine should measure up to the most absolute standards of technical excellence and, as a corollary, that havind done so, Negro medical mena and nurses should be accorded every opportunity to serve, without discrimination on account of race or color." July 19.
Benjamin Oliver Davis, Sr. was appointed Brigadier General, the first Black general in the history of the American armed forces. Oct. 16.

1941   George Washington Carver awarded the honorary Doctor of Science degree at the University of Rochester. June 18.
United States Supreme Court ruled in railroad Jim Crow case brought by Congressman Arthur Mitchell that separate facilities must be substantially equal. April 28.
Richard Wright, author, received Spingarn Medal because "he has given to Americans who have eyes to see a picture which must be faced if democracy is to survive . . . For his powerful depiction in his books, Uncle Tom's Children and Native Son, of the effect of proscription, segregation and denial of opportunities on the American Negro." June 27.
President Franklin D. Roosevelt established a Fair Employment Practices Commission. July 19.
Dorie Miller of Waco, Texas, messman on USS "Arizona," manned machine gun during Pearl Harbor attack and downed four enemy planes; later awarded Navy Cross. Dec. 7.

1942   Group of Negro and white men and women committed to direct non-violent action organized the Congress of Racial Equality in Chicago. June.
Bernard W. Robinson, Harvard Medical student, made an ensign in the United States Naval Reserve and was first Black to win a Commission in the United States Navy. June 18.
Spingarn Medal to A. Phillip Randolph, labor leader, international president of the Brotherhood of Sleeping Car Porters,

"for his unparalleled record of leadership in the field of
labor organization and national affairs for a period of more
than three decades . . . in recognition of the dramatic cul-
mination of his years of effort in the mobilization of Negro
mass opinion in 1941 in a March on Washington to exercise
the constitutional right of citizens of a democracy to petition
their government peaceably for the redress of grievances/
which/ was instrumental in securing the issuance on June 25,
1941, by the President of the United States of an executive
order banning discrimination on account of race, creed,
color, or national origin in defense industries and in the
federal government, and creating the Committee on Fair
Employment Practices to effectuate the order." July 19.
William L. Dawson elected to Congress from Chicago.
Nov. 3.

1943
Death of George Washington Carver in Tuskegee, Alabama.
Jan. 5.
George Gerswin's Porgy and Bess opened on Broadway star-
ring Anne Brown and Todd Duncan. Feb. 28.
Booker T. Washington was the first American merchant ship
commanded by a Black captain, High Malzoc, launched at
Wilmington, Delaware.
William H. Hastie, jurist and educator, awarded Spingarn
Medal "for his distinguished career as a jurist and as an
uncompromising champion of equal justice. His every act,
and particularly his protest against racial bigotry in an
army fighting for the democratic processes, has established
a standard of character and conduct." June 6.
Race riot in Detroit. Thirty-four killed; federal troops
called out. June 16.
Major race riot broke out in Harlem. Aug. 1-2.
Lt. Charles Hall, Brazil, Indiana, was first American
Black to shoot down Nazi plane. July 2.

1944
United States Supreme Court in Smith v. Allwright, banned
the "white primary" which had effectively prevented Blacks
in the South from voting. April 24.
United Negro College Fund established. April 24.
Dr. Mary E. Branch, president of Tillotson College, Austin,
Texas, died. July 8.
Spingarn Medal awarded to Dr. Charles R. Drew, scientist,
"for his outstanding work in blood plasma. Dr. Drew's research in this field led to the establishment of a blood
plasma bank which served as one of the models for the
widespread system of blood banks used by the American

Red Cross. Dr. Drew was appointed full-time Medical
Director for the blood plasma project for Great Britain.
The report on this work was published and served as a
guide for later developments for the United States Army
and for the armies of our Allies." July 16.
Death of composer Will Marion Cook. July 20.
Black historian Edward A. Johnson died. July 24.
Adam Clayton Powell elected first Black Congressman
from the East. Aug. 1.
Anna Lucasta, starring Hilda Simms and Frederick O'Neil,
opened on Broadway and was one of the year's great stage
successes. Aug. 20.
SS Frederick Douglass, first ship named for a Black, was
sunk by enemy action. Aug. 20.
Black servicewomen sworn into WAVES for first time.
Dec. 13.

1945   First state Fair employment Practices Commission was
established in New York State. March 12.
One thousand white students walked out of Gary, Indiana,
schools to protest school integration. Sept. 18.
Paul Robeson, singer and actor, received Spingarn Medal
for "distinguished achievement in the theatre and on the
concert stage." Oct. 18.
Irving C. Molleson, Chicago Republican, sworn in as
United States Customs Judge. Nov. 3.
More than one million Blacks were inducted or drafted into
the United States armed forces by the time World War II
ended.

1946   Countee Cullen, poet, died in New York City. Jan. 9.
William H. Hastie confirmed as governor of the Virgin
Islands. May 1.
Mrs. E. C. Clement first Black named "Mother of the Year."
May 1.
Supreme Court banned segregation in interstate bus travel.
June 3.
Thurgood Marshall, special counsel of the NAACP, given
Spingarn Medal for "his distinguished service as a lawyer
before the Supreme Court of the United States and inferior
courts, particularly in the Texas Primary Case, which
conceivably may have more far-reaching influence than
any other act in the ending of disfranchisement based upon
race or color in the country." June 28.

1947   Jackie Robinson joined the Brooklyn Dodgers, first Black
                in organized baseball in modern times. April 10.
                Dr. Percy L. Julian, research chemist, received the Sping-
                arn Medal "in recognition of his work as a distinguished
                chemist who has made many important discoveries that have
                saved many lives. He has demonstrated technical skill,
                courage and sustained effort on the highest level in making
                contributions that will benefit mankind for years to come."
                June 27.
                President's Committee on Civil Rights condemned racial
                injustices in America in a formal report, "To Secure These
                Rights." Oct. 29.

1948   First Lt. Nancy C. Leftenant was first Black accepted in the
                regular Army Nurse Corps. Feb. 12.
                United States Supreme Court declared restrictive housing
                covenants unenforceable in the courts (Shelly. v. Kraemer)
                May 3.
                Black elected for the first time to the American Nurses'
                Association Board of Directors. June 12.
                A. Philip Randolph formed the League for Non-Violent Civil
                Disobedience Against Military Segregation. June 26.
                Spingarn Medal awarded to Channing H. Tobias, "in recog-
                nition of his consistent role as a defender of fundamental
                American liberties . . . He brought to the President's Com-
                mittee on Civil Rights intellectual vitality, courage and the
                richness of his long experience in the field of race relations.
                Largely due to his persistence and clear insight the com-
                mittee produced a report of historic significance in man's
                unending struggle for justice." June 27.
                Poet Claude McKay died in Chicago.

1949   Congressman William L. Dawson became Chairman of
                House Expenditures Committee, the first Black to head a
                standing Committee in Congress. Jan. 18.
                Palisades, New Jersey, swimming pool integrated after two-
                year non-violent campaign. June 1.
                Wesley A. Brown was first Black to graduate from Annapolis
                Naval Academy. June 3.
                United States Navy Department announced policy of equality
                of treatment and opportunity to all persons in Navy and
                Marine Corps. June 7.
                Dr. Ralph J. Bunche, international civil servant, awarded
                Spingarn Medal "for his distinguished scholarship in the
                Myrdal study, his painstaking efforts as director of the
                United Nations Trusteeship Division, but principally for

his priceless contribution to the settlement of armed con-
flict in the Middle East." June 17.
Station W E R D was opened as the first Black owned radio
station in the United States in Atlanta, Georgia. Oct. 3.
William H. Hastie nominated for United States Circuit
Court of Appeals. Oct. 15.
Famed dancer Bill Robinson of stage and screen died in
New York City. Nov.25.

1950   James Weldon Johnson Memorial Collection of Black Arts
and Letters given to Yale University by Charles Van Vech-
ten. Jan. 8.
Dr. Charles R. Drew, pioneer in blood research, died.
April 1.
Death of Dr. Carter G. Woodson in Washington, D.C.
April 3.
Attorney-General MacGrath and Solicitor-General Perlman
argued before the U.S. Supreme Court for the reversal of
1896 ruling which upheld segregation. April 4.
Charles H. Houston, leading constitutional lawyer, died.
April 22.
While holding against segregation in the three cases before
it, the U.S. Supreme Court avoided general ruling on
"separate but equal" doctrine. June 6.
Spingarn Medal awarded posthumously to Charles H. Houston, Chairman, NAACP Legal Committee and "stalwart
defender of democracy, inspired teacher of youth, and
leader in the legal profession . . . in memory of a lifetime of gallant championship of equal rights for all Americans, of unselfish devotion to democratic ideals, of un-
swerving fidelity to the American dream of equal opportunity." June 25.
American Medical Association seated first Black delegate.
June 26.
Mrs. E. Sampson was first United States Black appointed
as representative to the United Nations. Aug. 19.
Dr. Ralph J. Bunche was the first American Black to receive the Nobel Peace Prize. Sept. 22.
Althea Gibson filed entry for national tennis championship;
first Negro accepted. Oct. 26.

1951   National Association of Colored Graduate Nurses disbanded
since aim to integrate Blacks into nursing profession
achieved. Jan. 27.
University of North Carolina admitted first Black student
in its history. April 24.

Oscar De Priest, former Congressman from Illinois, died. May 12.

Dr. Ralph J. Bunche first Black to win honorary degree from Princeton, New Jersey. June 13.

Spingarn Award to Mabel Keaton Staupers, who, as a leader of the National Association of Colored Nurses, "spearheaded the successful movement to integrate Black nurses into American life as equals," and whose work was "characterized by wisdom, vision, courage and refusal to equivocate," as a result of which the NACGN was dissolved as no longer needed. June 29.

Carver National Monument in Joplin, Missouri dedicated; first national park honoring Blacks. July 14.

Harry T. Moore, NAACP Coordinator for Florida, killed by bomb blast in house. Dect. 27.

Pfc. W. H. Thompson given Medal of Honor posthumously for Korean War action; first Black to receive this since Spanish-American War.

Riots in Cicero, Illinois, worst since 1919.

Martin Luther King, Jr. received the Bachelor of Divinity degree from Crozier Theological Seminary, Chester, Pennsylvania.

1952   University of Tennessee admitted its first Black student. Jan. 12.

Judge Waring quit his Charleston, South Carolina home as a result of ostracism for his fight for Blacks. Feb. 24.

Spingarn Medal awarded posthumously to Harry T. Moore, NAACP leader in the State of Florida, and a martyr in the "crusade for freedom," for "his invaluable contributions and his courage in working for full implementation of the democratic ideal," including justice in the courts, the abolition of segregation at the University of Florida, and the expansion of the Black vote in the state. Assassinated by a hate bomb in his home at Mims on Christmas night, 1951. June 27.

Ford Theatre of Baltimore dropped segregation policy in effect since 1861.

Southern Regional Council reported forty bombings since January 1951. Dec. 7.

Tuskegee Institute reported that 1952 was the first year in seventy-one years of tabulation that there were no reported lynchings. Dec. 30.

1953   Fisk was first Black institution of higher education in United States to get Phi Beta Kappa chapter. April 5.

United States Supreme Court ruled that District of Columbia
restaurants could not legally refuse to serve Blacks. June 8.
Albert W. Dent of Dillard University was elected President
of the National Health Council. June 20.
NAACP set intergregation as goal, dropped "separate but
equal" theory. June 23.
Paul R Williams, distinguished architect, awarded Spingarn
Medal for his pioneer contributions as a creative designer
of livable and attractive modern dwellings and beautiful utili-
tarian commercial structures--contributions which have won
for him the respect and admiration of his fellow architects
and high rank in his chosen profession. June 26.
Drama by Black playwright Louis Peterson, Take a Giant
Step, opened on Broadway. Sept. 24.
Hulan Jack elected president of the Borough of Manhattan.
Nov. 4.

1954   J. Ernest Wilkins of Chicago appointed Assistant Secretary
of Labor by President Dwight Eisenhower, April 23.
Landmark United States Supreme Court case, Brown v.
Board of Education, et al. declared that racial segregation
in public schools was unconstituional. May 17.
White Brotherhood set up in Georgia to retain segregation.
June 6.
E. L. Ashford of Pacific Coast League was first Black umpire
in organized baseball. June 13.
Spingarn Medal to Theodore K. Lawless, physician, edu-
cator, and philanthropist, recognized as one of the world's
leading dermatologists, for his extensive research and ex-
periments which have enlarged the area of scientific know-
ledge in his chosen field. July 4.
First White Citizens Council unit was organized in Indianola,
Mississippi. July 11.
Charles V. Bush was first Black page boy in Supreme Court
and first in Capitol page school. July 24.
Mary Church Terrell died in Washington, D.C. July 24.
Dr. F. M. Snowden appointed cultural attache in embassy
in Rome; first Black in major embassy post. Aug. 19.
S. Richardson named Chairman of the Federal Parole Board;
first Black on Board. Sept. 29.
Benjamin Davis, Jr. appointed first Black general in the Air
Force. Oct. 27.
Defense Department announced all units in the armed forces
were now integrated. Oct. 30.
Carol Williams engaged by Sadler Wells Opera. Nov. 26.
Track star M. Whitman first Black to win Sullivan Tropy,
top United States amateur award. Dec. 31.

1955   Marian Anderson made her debut at the Metropolitan Opera
            House; she was the first Black singer in the company's his-
            tory. Jan. 7.
            Charlie Parker, one of the founders of the modern jazz move-
            ment, died. March 12.
            Death of Walter White, NAACP leader, in New York City.
            March 21.
            Roy Wilkins appointed Executive Secretary of NAACP.
            April 11.
            Mrs. Mary McLeod Bethune died in Daytona Beach, Florida.
            May 18.
            U.S. Supreme Court decree for the implementation of the
            May 17, 1954, school desegregation decision; "with all due
            and deliberate speed." May 31.
            Spingarn Medal awarded to Carl Murphy, dedicated editor,
            publisher and far-sighted civic leader, for his leadership
            role in 'veling invidious racial barriers in employment,
            education and recreation. June 26.
            E. F. Morrow appointed administrative officer in the Eisen-
            hower Executive Office. July 8.
            Georgia Education Board ordered lifetime ban on teachers
            who instructed "mixed" classes. July 11.
            Emmet Till, fourteen years old, was kidnapped and lynched
            in Money, Mississippi. Aug. 28.
            Interstate Commerce Commission banned segregation in
            buses, waiting rooms and travel coaches involved in inter-
            state travel. Nov. 25.
            Bus boycott initiated in Montgomery, Alabama. Dec. 5.

1956   Autherine Lucy admitted to University of Alabama. Feb. 3.
            National Press Club admitted L. R. Lautier as first Black.
            Feb. 5.
            Miss Lucy suspended after riot at University of Alabama.
            Feb. 7.
            Manifest denouncing U.S. Supreme Court ruling on segre-
            gation in public schools was issued by one hundred Southern
            Senators and Representatives. March 11-12.
            U.S. Supreme Court banned segregation in public parks,
            playgrounds, beaches and golf courses; rejected "separate
            but equal" doctrine.
            Leontyne Price was first Black to sing before mixed audience
            in Laurel, Mississippi.
            Louisville, Kentucky, schools integrated. Sept. 10.
            Dr. John Hope Franklin appointed chairman of the history
            department at Brooklyn College.
            Jack ("Jackie") R. Robinson, brilliant and versatile athlete,

received Spingarn Medal for "his superb sportsmanship, his pioneer role in opening up a new field of endeavor for young Blacks, and his civic consciousness." Dec. 8.

1957   Martin Luther King, Jr. elected president of Southern Christian Leadership Conference at its organization meeting in New Orleans. Jan. 12.

Robert Ming, Chicago lawyer, elected Chairman of American Veterans Committee, first Black to head major national veterans organization. April 28.

Spingarn Medal awarded to Martin Luther King, Jr., dedicated and selfless clergyman, for his creative contributions to the Fight for Freedom and his outstanding leadership role in the successful Montgomery bus protest movement. June 28.

Althea Gibson won women's Single Championship at Wimbledom, England and the United States Law Tennis Championship. July 7, 22.

Booker T. Washington National Monument opened at Rocky Mount, Virginia; second such memorial to a Black leader. July 28.

Rev. A. J. Carey, Jr. appointed Chairman of President's Government Employment Policy Committee; first Black in this position. Aug. 6.

Prayer Pilgrimage, the largest civil rights demonstration staged by American Blacks up to that time, held in Washington, D.C.

Congress passed the first Civil Rights Act since 1875. Aug. 29.

President Eisenhower ordered federal troops to Little Rock, Arkansas, to prevent interference with school integration at Central High School. Sept. 24.

New York City was first to legislate against racial or religious discrimination in housing with the adoption of its Fair Housing Practice law. Dec. 5.

1958   Clifton R. Wharton confirmed as Minister to Rumania. Feb. 5.

Mrs. Daisy Bates and the Little Rock Nine awarded Spingarn Medal for "their pioneer role in upholding the basic ideal of American democracy in the face of continuing harassment and constant threats of bodily injury." July 11.

Members of NAACP Youth Council began series of sit-ins at Oklahoma City lunch counters. Aug. 19.

1959   First play written by a Black woman, <u>Raisin in the Sun</u>, by
            Lorraine Hansberry, was one of the major Broadway hits.
            March 11.
            Second "Youth March for Integrated Schools" drew 30,000
            students to Washington, D.C. April 18.
            Mack Parker lynched in Poplarville, Mississippi. April 25.
            Prince Edward County, Virginia, Board of Supervisors aban-
            doned public school system in attempt to prevent school seg-
            regation. June 26.
            Rev. Dr. King and others urged President Eisenhower to
            make statement against segregation. July 5.
            Billie Holiday, leading blues singer, died in New York City.
            July 17.
            Dade County, Florida, first to desegregate public schools
            in Florida.
            Spingarn Medal given to Edward Kennedy (Duke) Ellington,
            composer and orchestra leader, for his outstanding musical
            achievements which have won for him "not only universal
            acclaim but also worldwide recognition of our country's con-
            tribution to the field of music." Sept. 11.
            Citizens of Deerfield, Illinois, authorized plan which blocked
            building of interracial housing development. Dec. 21.

1960   Forty-three arrested in Raleigh, North Carolina, sit-in.
            Feb. 10.
            Fifty-nine arrested in Chatanooga, Tennessee, sit-in. Feb.
            19.
            Pope John elevated Bishop Laurian Rugambwa of Tanganyika
            to College of Cardinals, first Black Cardinal in modern
            times. March 3.
            Students served at Salisbury, North Carolina and at Atlanta,
            Georgia, lunch counters; students demonstrated in New Or-
            leans. March 7.
            Three hundred and fifty protestors arrested and placed in
            stockade in Orangeburg, South Carolina. March 15.
            Forty arrested in sit-ins in four North Carolina cities.
            March 17.
            Thirty-seven Blacks arrested in public libraries in Memphis,
            Tennessee. March 19.
            Twenty-three arrested in art gallery and library in Mem-
            phis. March 22.
            Lunch counters integrated in Corpus Christi, Texas; six-
            teen students arrested in Baton Rouge, Louisiana. March
            28.
            Ten arrested in Birmingham sit-in; White House Conference

on Children and Youth endorsed sit-ins. March 31.
Student Non-Violent Coordinating Committee organized on
Shaw University campus. April 15.
Sit-in protest at chain stores in Savannah, Georgia; fifteen
arrested picketing chain stores in Ann Arbor, Michigan.
April 16.
United States Federal Court ruled that Atlanta, Georgia,
must start school segregation by September, 1961. May 9.
Winston-Salem lunch counters integrated. May 25.
Four lunch counters integrated in Oak Ridge, Tennessee,
June 4.
Langston Hughes, poet, author and playwright, received
Spingarn Medal in recognition of his reputation "in America,
Europe, Asia, Africa, Central and South America as a major
American writer and considered by many the poet laureate
of the Negro race." June 26.
Democratic National Convention adopted Civil Rights plank
supporting sit-ins and school integration. July 12.
Elijah Muhammad, black internationalist leader, called for
creation of Black state at New York City meeting. July 31.
Southern Regional Council reported that eight cities that
desegregated lunch counters maintained "sales as usual."
Southern School News reported that 94% of Blacks in Amer-
ica were attending segregated schools.
During decade of 1950-1960, 1,500,000 Blacks migrated
from South to Northern communities.
Richard Wright died in Paris. Nov. 28.

1961   Adam Clayton Powell assumed the Chairmanship of the Edu-
            cation and Labor Committee of the House of Representatives.
            Jan. 3.
            Carl T. Rowan appointed Deputy Assistant Secretary of
            State for Public Affairs. Jan. 25.
            H. Lewis conducted Los Angeles Philharmonic Orchestra;
            first Black to conduct major symphony orchestra at its home
            during the regular season. Feb. 10.
            Robert Weaver sworn in as Administrator of Housing and
            Home Finance Agency, highest federal post ever held by
            an American Black. Feb. 11.
            Thirteen "Freedom Riders" began bus trip through the
            South. May 4.
            Soprano Leontyne Price starred in Metropolitan Opera Com-
            pany's Girl of the Golden West, first Black to open Met season
            in leading role. May 24.
            Marvin Cook named ambassador to Niger Republic; first
            Black envoy named by Kennedy Administration to African
            nation. May 26.

C. F. Poole appointed Attorney for Northern California District; first Black in such position appointed in continental United States. April 16.

Jacksonville, Florida, closed its swimming pool to avoid integration. June 13.

Gene Baker, former 2nd baseman for Pittsburgh Pirates, was first Black ex-major leaguer to advance to position of major league farm team. June 20.

Ten "Freedom Riders" sentenced in Tallahasse Airport case. June 23.

George L. P. Weaver named Secretary of Labor in charge of international affairs. July 9.

Spingarn Medal awarded to Kenneth B. Clark, Professor of Psychology at the College of the City of New York; founder and director of the Northside Center for Child Development and prime mobilizer of the resources of modern psychology in the attack upon racial segregation, for his dedicated service and inspired research which contributed significantly to the historic U.S. Supreme Court decision of May 17, 1954, banning segregation in public education. July 16.

President John F. Kennedy nominated Thurgood Marshall to the United States Circuit Court of Appeals. Sept. 23.

Otis Marion Smith became Associate Justice on the Michigan Supreme Court. Oct. 10.

Cincinnati Reds outfielder, Frank Robinson, voted "Most Valuable Player" of the year by Baseball Writers' Association. Nov. 23.

James H. Meredith registered at the University of Mississippi.

United Press International picked Chicago Cubs' outfielder, Billy Williams, as the National League's "Rookie of the Year.'

Ernie Davis of Syracuse University was first Black to win Harmon Trophy as college football's "Player of the Year."

American Anthropological Association reaffirmed belief in inherent equality of Blacks and whites. Nov. 21.

Blacks comprised 12% of population in cities of over 1,000,000, compared with 10% of a decade ago. Dec. 3.

In a final blow to "massive resistance," United States courts held unconstitutional a law permitting closing of integration-ordered public school districts.

There was an increase of 17,907 students, or 6% in the South's Black attendance of mixed classes over 1960.

School board presidencies of Oakland, California, and Washington, D.C. went to Blacks, the first Blacks to lead school systems in major United States metropolitan centers.

John Duncan became first Black to serve as Commissioner for Washington, D.C.

Chicago Human Relations Commission reported city's Black population rose from 492,265 to 812,637, in the decade from 1950 to 1960.
1960 Census showed that 1,087,931 Blacks resided in New York City; 14% of city's total population and the largest number of Blacks of any city in the United States.

1962   Jackie Robinson was first Black to be elected to National Baseball Hall of Fame. Jan. 24.
Lt. Commander Samuel L. Gravely given command of destroyer escort, USS Falgout; first Black to command U.S. warship. Jan. 31.
Mattiwilda Dobbs became first person (Negro or white) to sing before integrated audience in Municipal Hall in Atlanta, Georgia. Feb. 1.
John Thomas appointed Director of the Health, Education and Welfare Department's Cuban Refugee Program. March 15.
Census Bureau reported 6,025,173 of 18,871,831 Blacks lived in 25 largest cities; 1,457,000 Blacks migrated from South to northern and western regions in last decade. April 15.
Johnson Publishing Company was first Black company to enter book publishing field. April 25.
Luke C. Moore became first U.S. Marshal since Frederick Douglass held such position. May 9.
John Hope Franklin appointed William Pitt Professor of American History and Institutions at Cambridge University, England, for one year. May 20.
Death of E. Franklin Frazier, noted sociologist and historian, after 45 years of teaching. May 22.
J. O'Neill named Chicago Cubs coach; first Black coach in major leagues. May 30.
W. W. Braithwaite, poet, anthologist and literary critic, died in New York City. June 9.
Big Bill Russell of the Boston Celtics named "Player of the Year" by Sporting News. June 19.
NAACP had more cases before the U.S. Supreme Court than any institution except the federal government. June 18.
Rev. W. E. Houston was first Black elected Moderator of United Presbyterian Church, N.Y. Synod. June 21.
Robert C. Weaver, Administrator, Housing and Home Finance Agency, awarded Spingarn Medal for his long years of dedicated public service at municipal, state and federal levels; for his pioneer role in the development and advocacy of the doctrine of "open occupancy" in housing; and for his responsible and militant leadership in the struggle for human rights. July 8.

Rev. Martin Luther King, Jr. arrested in Albany, Georgia, after anti-segregation demonstration. July 10.

Howard Jenkins, law professor at Howard University, appointed first Black member of the National Labor Relations Board. July 22.

Mel Goode was first Black TV news commentator on network TV (ABC-TV). Aug. 29.

U. S. Supreme Court ruled that University of Mississippi must admit James H. Meredith, a Black Air Force veteran, whose application for admission had been on file for 14 months. Sept. 10.

Hobart Taylor, Jr. appointed Executive Vice-Chairman of the President's Equal Opportunity Committee. Sept. 11.

Mississippi Governor Ross R. Barnett personally denied James H. Meredith admission to University of Mississippi. Sept. 20.

U.S. Circuit Court of Appeals ordered Board of Higher Education of Mississippi to admit Meredith to the University or face contempt charges; Board agreed to comply with order. Sept. 24.

Governor Barnett defied orders of Court and personally interfered with Meredith's attempt to enter the University to register. Sept. 25.

A. Leon Higginbotham nominated as federal judge for eastern Pennsylvania, youngest member of the federal bench in the U.S. Sept. 26.

Thurgood Marshall confirmed as member of Second United States Circuit Court of Appeals after one year delay by Southern opposition in U.S. Senate. Sept. 12.

Four major TV advertisers approved use of Black models in commercials aimed at nation-wide audience.

James Meredith escorted to the campus of the University of Mississippi with Federal Marshals. Sept. 30.

University of Mississippi students and adults from Oxford, Mississippi, and other Southern communities rioted on campus; two killed.

Federal soldiers restored order on campus and in town. Oct. 1.

Accompanied by federal marshals, James Meredith registered at the University. Oct.

Edward W. Brooke elected Attorney General of Massachusetts. Nov. 7.

August Hawkins elected as U.S. Representative from California, first Negro to represent this state. Nov. 7.

Leroy Johnson first Black state legislator elected in Georgia since Reconstruction. Nov. 8.

Gerald Lamb elected Connecticut State Treasurer. Nov. 8.
U.S. Supreme Court ruled that segregation in interstate and
intra state travel was unconstitutional.
Diahann Carroll was first black to play romantic lead in an
otherwise all- white Broadway musical, Richard Rodgers'
No Strings. April 15.
Maury Wills of the Los Angeles Dodgers broke all records
in major league baseball as the greatest "baseball thief"
(stolen bases).
Wilt Chamberlain of the San Francisco Warriors was first
professional basketball player to score 4000 points in a
single season.
2000 Blacks were enrolled in previously "whites only" colleges and universities in the South.
There were 948 "token-integrated" public school districts
in the all-white southern school districts, an increase of
124 districts over 1961.
Archbishop Joseph F. Rummel directed all Roman Catholic
schools in his Louisiana archdiocese to integrate.
Marjorie Lawson became first Black woman judge in Washington, D.C.
Mrs. Ann Roberts appointed FHA Deputy Regional Administrator and became highest ranking Black woman in the federal housing field.
Fourteen Southern airports voluntarily integrated their pas-
senger facilities.
The Albany (Georgia) Movement, comprising the civil rights
efforts of several action groups, including CORE, SNCC,
SCLC, and the NAACP resulted in the following achievements
in social relations: (1) agreement by local authorities to
form a bi-racial committee on racial problems; (2) desegregation of the city's bus terminal and cafe; (3) release from
jail of movement demonstrators and an end to mass arrests;
(4) the substitution of "Mr. & Mrs." for derogatory terms
by city officials in addressing Negro citizens.
U.S. Supreme Court authorized Tennessee citizens to sue
in federal courts to force reapportionment of legislative
districts. This would result in shift of political power from
rural segregationist strongholds to the relatively more
liberal, heavily Black-populated urban South.

1963   James Baldwin's The Fire Next Time published. Jan. 31
President John F. Kennedy sent his Civil Rights Message
to Congress. March 1.
Carl T. Rowan appointed Ambassador to Finland. March 9.
John Thomas appointed Director of the Health, Education,

and Welfare Department's Cuban Refugee Program. March 15.

Dr. John Hope Franklin appointed to the faculty of the University of Chicago. April 14.

Arthur Ashe, 19, was first Black to join the U.S. Davis Cup Tennis Team. May 14.

U.S. Supreme Court ruled that in cities making segregation a matter of public policy, whether by ordinance or executive order, Blacks may not be prosecuted for seeking service in privately owned stores. May 21.

President Kennedy said nation faced "moral crisis" over Black demands for equality; pledged legislation to open public facilities for all (TV address). June 12.

Spingarn Medal awarded to Medgar Wile Evers, NAACP Field Secretary for the State of Mississippi, World War II veteran, hero and martyr felled by an assassin's bullet in the back on June 12; accepted posthumously by his wife. July 4.

Largest civil rights demonstration in history took place at the site of the Lincoln and Washington Memorial in Washington, D.C.; 250,000 persons participated. Aug. 29.

Bomb exploded in Birmingham Negro Baptist Church killing four Black girls; two Black youths killed in racial rioting which followed. Sept. 6.

James W. Silver, Professor of History at the University of Mississippi and retiring President of the Southern Historical Association, charged that Mississippi is "a closed society and a century behind culturally." Nov. 8.

Rev. Benjamin J. Anderson, pastor of Princeton's historic Witherspoon Street Presbyterian Church, was nominated to become the first Black to serve as a moderator of the General Assembly of the United Presbyterian Church. Nov. 30.

Ralph J. Bunche and Marian Anderson were among the recipients of Medals of Freedom from President L. B. Johnson at the White House. Dec. 7.

Dinah Washington died. Dec. 14.

Outfielder Tommy Davis of the Los Angeles Dodgers won baseball's batting crown for the 2nd consecutive year.

William T. Mason Jr. appointed first Black Assistant Federal Attorney in Virginia.

1964   Senator Barry Goldwater called public accommodations section of the Civil Rights Act unconstitutional. Jan. 19.

Carl T. Rowan appointed Director of the United States Information Agency, the highest position ever held by a Black in the federal government. Jan. 21.

Atlanta Constitution, a leading Southern newspaper, reversed
a previous position and editorially supported the public ac-
commodations provision of the Civil Rights Act. Jan. 22.
Beckworth trial for murder of Medgar Evers opened. Feb. 1.
A. T. Walden sworn in as Atlanta municipal judge; first
Black judge in Georgia since Reconstruction. Feb. 4.
Mistrial in Beckworth trial; jury unable to agree. Feb. 8.
Race riot in Jacksonville, Florida. March 24-26.
U.S. Supreme Court set aside contempt conviction of Black
Mary Hamilton who declined to answer in Alabama court
when addressed as "Mary." March 31.
Second jury unable to agree in Beckworth case; mistrial de-
clared. April 26.
U. S. Supreme Court ruled that Prince Edward County in
Virginia must re-open its public schools on an integrated
basis. May 26.
Sidney Poitier won the Academy of Motion Picture Arts and
Sciences' Oscar Award as best actor of 1963 for his per-
formance in Lilies of the Field. April.
Three civil rights workers reported missing on Mississippi
Sumer Project two weeks after release from jail in Phila-
delphia, Mississippi. June 23.
Spingarn Medal awarded to Roy Wilkins, Executive Secre-
tary of the NAACP, "despite his own urgent request that this
present honor not be conferred upon him," for the "distinctive
and immeasurable contribution to the advancement of the
American people and the national purpose" in his work on
behalf of civil rights movement." June 23.
Race riots in Rochester, New York. July 1.
Civil Rights Act of 1964 passed and signed into law; most
far-reaching civil rights legislation since Civil War Amend-
ments. July 3.
Fifteen year old Black James Powell shot and killed by off-
duty police Lt. Gilligan in New York City. July 17.
Race riot in Harlem. July 19.
Bodies of civil rights workers Goodman, Schwerner and
Chaney found in newly-built earthen dam near Philadelphia,
Mississippi. Aug. 5.
Race riots in South Chicago suburb in Dixmoor; 50 hurth.
Aug. 17-18.
Philadelphia race riots; 29 hurt. Aug. 29-30.
FBI arrested four Philadelphia, Mississippi, law enforce-
ment officers and former sheriff in connection with murder
of three civil rights workers. Oct. 4.
Rev. Martin Luther King, Jr. won Nobel Peace Prize. Oct.
15.

NAACP resumed operations in Alabama for first time since enjoined from operating in state in 1956. Nov. 1.

Negro Baptist Church burned near Ripley, Mississippi. Nov. 1.

Civil Rights struggle in Mississippi has resulted in: three killed, eighty beaten, three wounded by gunfire, over one thousand arrested, thirty-five churches burned, thirty-one homes and other buildings bombed--since the beginning of the year 1964.

Jackson District Attorney announced Beckworth will not be tried for murder of Medgar Evers without new evidence. Nov. 15.

U.S. Supreme Court upheld the constitutionality of the public accommodations section of the Civil Rights Act of 1964. Dec.

Public schools of the District of Columbia were registering a pupil enrollment of 85.7% Black.

Ford Foundation announced grants totalling $15,000,000 to strengthen Black colleges.

Hampton Institute opened its new Communications Center, marking the 125th anniversary of the birth of the founder of Hampton, Samuel C. Armstrong.

Senator Richard B. Russell (Georgia) proposed a voluntary relocation of Blacks proportionately at government expense throughout the states of the federal union.

Arthur B. Spingarn, a founder of NAACP and President since 1940, announced plans to retire at the end of the year.

Erwin S. Perry, who received his Ph.D.. this year from the University of Texas, made such a distinguished record that he was appointed to the University faculty commencing in September.

Hobart Taylor appointed Associate Special Counsel at the White House for President L.B. Johnson, succeeding Theodore C. Sorenson.

National Urban League launched anti-poverty campaign among Blacks under leadership of Whitney Young, Jr.

Clinton E. Knox nominated Ambassador to Dahomey.

John Haynes Holmes, one of founders of NAACP, died.

Three Broadway shows included interracial romances without audience incident: Golden Boy, The Sign in Sidney Brustein's Window, The Owl and the Pussycat.

Black athletes contributed significantly to United States pres-
tige at the XVIII Olympics in Tokyo by winning half of the 36
gold medals awarded American athletes.

1965   Lorraine Vivian Hansberry, leading Black playwright, died
in New York City. Jan. 13.
President Lyndon B. Johnson appointed Lisle Carter, a Black,
as Assistant Secretary in the Department of Health, Education and Welfare. Jan. 15.
Three men indicted for beating Black civil rights worker in
Greenwood, Mississippi, were the first persons to be arrested under the Civil Rights Act of 1964. Jan. 15.
Survey of N. Y. Times of compliance with Civil Rights Act
showed substantial compliance with Title II (Public Accommodations) in South, but "painfully slow progress against
voting discrimination under Title I." Jan. 16.
Constance Baker Motley, former President of the Borough
of Manhattan in New York City, became first Black woman
to be appointed to a federal judgeship. Jan. 25.
Governor Edward Breathitt of Kentucky signed Civil Rights
law, first of its kind adopted by any state south of the Ohio
River. Jan. 25.
Geraldine McCullough was the first Black winner of the Wid-
ener Memorial Medal for Sculpture, awarded by the Pennsylvania Academy of Fine Arts. Feb. 3.
United States Civil Rights Commission reported that majority
of Southern school districts were evading integration while
still adhering to federal guidelines for desegregation. Feb.
15.
Nat "King" Cole, noted singing artist, died in Los Angeles.
Feb. 16.
Malcolm X was assassinated in New York City while addressing rally of his followers. Feb. 22.
Wyatt T. Walker, former assistant to Dr. Martin Luther
King, Jr., named Special Assistant on Urban Affairs to Gov-
ernor Nelson Rockefeller of New York. March 1.
Bill Russell of the Boston Celtics was honored as the most
valuable player in the National Basketball Association for
the fourth time in five years. March 4.
Federal Judge authorized Selma-Montgomery march in Ala-
bama. March 17.
President Lyndon B. Johnson called up 4,000 troops to protect Selma-Montgomery marchers. March 18.
Dr. Martin Luther King, Jr. and Under-Secretary of United
Nations Ralph Bunche lead 3,200 on 54 mile Selma-Montgomery march. March 21.

March from Selma ended as 25,000 Blacks and whites rallied
in front of capitol, Montgomery, March 25.
Mrs. Crystal Bird Fauset, pioneer female legislator, died.
March 30.
The first Black city councilman in the history of San Antonio,
Texas, was elected when Rev. S. H. James defeated three
candidates. April 8.
St. Thomas Episcopal Church of Philadelphia voted to nullify
its 1796 charter restriction that limited membership to
"Africans and descendants of African race." April 11.
Soprano Leontyne Price was awarded the Order of Merit of
the Italian Republic. April 13.
Bishop Prince A. T. Taylor, Jr. became the first Black to
assume the presidency of the Council of Bishops of the Meth-
odist Church. April 23.
J. Raymond Jones elected leader of the powerful New York
County Democratic Committee (Tammany Hall). May 22.
Lerone Bennett, Jr., Senior Editor of Ebony Magazine, was
awarded the 1965 Patron Saints Award Society of Midland
Authors for his biography of Dr. Martin Luther King, Jr.,
What Manner of Man. June 17.
President Lyndon B. Johnson issued Executive Order creating
cabinet-level Council on Equal Opportunity, with Vice-President Humphrey as Chairman, to coordinate civil rights ac-
tivities of all federal agencies. July 7.
The 1965 Voting Rights Act, providing for the registration
by federal examiners of those Black voters turned away by
state officials, signed by President Lyndon B. Johnson.

1966   Arthur B. Spingarn retired as President of NAACP after
serving since 1940. Jan. 3.
Robert C. Henry unanimously elected mayor of Springfield,
Ohio, by City Council, the first Black to become mayor of
an Ohio city. Jan. 3.
Floyd B. McKissick appointed National Director of CORE,
Jan. 4.
H. B. Perry installed as Auxillary Bishop of New Orleans,
first Black to hold that position in the United States since
1875. Jan. 7.
Bertram L. Baker became Assembly Majority Whip in the
New York State legislature, first Black to win a leadership
position in the state's legislature. Jan. 10.
Robert C. Weaver appointed by President L. B. Johnson as
Secretary of Housing and Urban Development, first Black to
serve in a President's Cabinet. Jan. 14.

The United Negro College Fund received a grant of $2,000,000 from United States Steel Corporation.

Andrew Brimmer appointed to the Federal Reserve Banking Board, first Black to serve on the Board. Feb. 27.

Announcement was made that the new Smithsonian Institute in Washington, D.C., will hand in the Hall of Historic Americans in the Museum of History and Technology exhibits illustrating the progress of the civil rights movement from the earliest slave days to the March on Washington in 1963.

United States Supreme court upheld major provisions of 1965 Voting Rights Act, rejecting contention of Southern states that voting qualifications were powers reserved to states. March 7

Hundreds of Black teen-agers rioted in 12-square block area in Watts district of Los, Angeles, California. March 16

United States Supreme Court ruled Virginia poll tax unconstitutional, thereby ending poll tax in three other Southern states. March 25

United States Census Bureau reported Cook County, Illinois, had the largest Black population of any county in the United States: 861, 146. March 26

Bill (William F.) Russell named as Boston Celtics basketball coach, first Black to direct major American professional sports team. March 28

First World Festival of Black Arts was held in Dakar, Senegal. April 1-24

Pfc. M.L. Olive was the first Black to receive the Congressional Medal of Honor in the Vietnam War. April 22

John Lewis was defeated for re-election as Chairman of the Student Nonviolent Coordinating Committee (SNCC) by Stokely Carmichael, reflecting SNCC move to deemphasize whites' role in civil rights activities. May 16

White House Civil Rights Conference issued recommendations calling for multi-billion dollar program to give Blacks "true equality." May 25

Eliot P. Skinner confirmed by United States Senate as Ambassador to Upper Volta, Africa. May 29

Stephen J. Wright resigned as President of Fisk University to become President of the United Negro College Fund. June 2

James H. Meredith began 200-mile civil rights march from Memphis, Tennesse to Jackson, Mississippi, to encourage voter registration among Blacks in the South. June 6

Meredith was shot in the back from ambush near Hernando, Mississippi. June 7.

National convention of Congress of Racial Equality (CORE)
voted to adopt resolution endorsing concept of "black power"
as enunciated by Stokely Carmichael during the Meredith
March. July 1.

NAACP disassociated itself from the "Black Power" doctrine.
July 4.

Dr. Martin Luther King, Jr., launched drive to make Chicago an "open city." July 10.

Three nights of rioting swept Chicago's West Side Black
district. July 12-15.

Shooting, fire-bombing and looting in the Black area of
Hough on Cleveland's East Side. July 18-23.

Dr. Martin Luther King, Jr., stoned in Chicago while leading march in Gage Park section of Chicago's Southwest Side.
Aug. 5.

New York Assemblyman Percy Sutton elected President of
the Borough of Manhattan. Sept. 13.

Emmet T. Rice was appointed United States Alternate-
Executive Director of the World Bank. Oct. 18.

Edward W. Brooke elected United States Senator in Massachusetts on the Republican ticket; the first Black Senator
since Reconstruction. Nov. 9.

House of Representatives denied Adam Clayton Powell his
Congressional seat until Select Committee probed and reported on his qualifications. Jan. 10.

Twenty Governors proclaimed Negro History Week. Feb.
14.

President L. B. Johnson proposed new Federal Civil Rights
Act of 1967. Feb. 16.

Nineteen men, including a County Sheriff and KKK Imperial
Wizard were indicted under felony provisions of 1870 Civil
Rights statute in connection with death of three civil rights
workers. March 1.

House of Representatives, 207-116, voted to exclude Adam
Clayton Powell. March 2.

The Negro National Business & Professional Committee was
organized at the Harvard Club in New York City; consisted
of 47 business and professional Black leaders who plan to
raise $1,000,000 annually to subsidize the Legal & Educa-
tion Fund of the NAACP. March 24.

Dr. Martin Luther King, Jr., announced he would take
strong stand against Vietnam War because it was major
obstacle to Civil Rights movement. March 24.

Texas Legislature passed first civil rights act in recent
history. April 6.

Roman Catholic priest Rev. Joseph Groppi charged with

obstructing police and resisting arrest during disturbances following meeting of Milwaukee NAACP Youth Council of which he is advisor. May 7.

Blacks of Roxbury section in Boston rioted in protest against Department of Welfare treatment. June 4.

Blacks rioted in downtown Tampa, Florida, looting and setting block afire; 500 National Guardsmen called in by Governor. June 12.

United States Supreme Court upheld contempt of court conviction of Rev. Dr. Martin Luther King, Jr., and seven other ministers for violating order against leading desegregation protests in Birmingham, Alabama. June 14.

Blacks rioted in Cincinnatti, Ohio; Governor ordered 900 National Guardsmen to join 900 policemen. June 15.

Rev. E. H. Evans nominated for United Church of Christ national secretary, first Black to be nominated. June 24.

Fourteen persons shot, 1500 Black youths rioted in Buffalo, N.Y. June 30.

James Meredith completed second march to Canton, Mississippi, to prove that state and local police can protect Blacks if they choose. July 5.

United States Supreme Court unanimously outlawed antimiscegantion laws. June 12.

United States Senator Edward R. Brooke of Massachusetts received Annual Spingarn Medal of the NAACP for distinguished achievement. July 10.

Band of Blacks rioted in Newark, New Jersey; 11 persons killed. July 13.

SNCC Chairman "Rap" Brown slightly wounded after firey speech in Cambridge, Maryland, urging Blacks to burn town unless Black demands met. July 25.

Thousands of Blacks rioted throughout Detroit, Michigan. July 24.

President L. B. Johnson sent 4,700 army paratroopers into Detroit to deal with rioting. July 25.

National Guard fired on snipers as death toll in Detroit reached 36, more than the number slain in the 1965 Watts riot. July 27.

President Lyndon B. Johnson appointed 11-member committee headed by Governor Otto Kerner of Illinois and Mayor John Lindsay of New York to study causes and propose solutions to racial riots. July 28.

National Guard and United States Army withdrew from Detroit. July 29.

Mrs. Elizabeth D. Koontz was elected President of the National Education Association, the largest professional organization in the world. July.

The Baltimore Afro-American celebrated its 175th anniversary. August.

James Nabrit, Jr., resigned as President of Howard University in Washington, D.C. after a series of confrontations with Black militants on campus.

Carl Stokes was elected Mayor of Cleveland, Ohio. Nov. 9.

Richard G. Hatch was elected Mayor of Gary, Indiana. Nov. 9.

United States Senate confirmed the appointment of Thurgood Marshall as the first Black Associate Justice of the United States Supreme Court. Sept.

President Lyndon B. Johnson signed bill extending life of Civil Rights Commission to January, 1973. Dec. 16.

Maryland Constitutional Convention approved ban on racial discrimination. Dec. 26.

Brandeis University Lemberg Institute of Study of Violence announced that only five of two hundred disturbances that occured in 1967 appeared to have been precipitated by outside agitators. Dec. 29.

1968   About 100 Black leaders representing 20 organizations held a secret meeting in Washington, D.C. and formed a coalition "Black United Front," to organize Blacks in the nation's capital. Jan. 9.

Henry Lewis became the first Black appointed music director of a symphony orchestra in the United States, the New Jersey Symphony. Feb. 15.

For the first time in modern Alabama history, two Black candidates became the party's delegates to the Democratic National Convention. Feb. 26.

The President's National Advisory Commission on Civil Disorders issued its reports on the causes of racial riots in the summer of 1967. March 2.

Affirming a 1966 Federal District Court decision, the United States Supreme Court unanimously ruled that Alabama must desegregate its prisons within a year. The Court rejected Alabama's contention that segregation was necessary to maintain order. March 11.

The first state-wide open-housing law in the South became law in Tennessee after nearly a year of demonstrations in Memphis. March 27.

Black separatists met in Detroit for a National Black Conference sponsored by the Malcolm X Society to "set up an independent Black government" in five Southern states, and to write a "Black Declaration of Independence." March 30.

Martin Luther King, Jr., was assassinated in Memphis,

Tennessee, while preparing a march on behalf of striking
sanitation workers. April 4.
Widespread violence struck 125 cities following the assassi-
nation of Martin Luther King, Jr.; thirty-eight people were
killed and 20,000 arrested. Fifty-thousand Federal and
State troops were on duty throughout the country. April 5-11.
President L. B. Johnson declared a day of mourning in honor
of Martin Luther King, Jr. April 7.
Mrs. Coretta King, Dr. King's widow, elected to Board of
Directors of Southern Christian Leadership Conference
(SCLC); Dr. Ralph D. Abernathy was elected president.
April 9.
Civil Rights Act of 1968 featuring provisions to eliminate
racial barriers in the nation's housing programs was passed
by Congress. April 10.
A settlement was reached in the Memphis, Tennessee,
sanitation men's strike; the cause that had brought Martin
Luther King, Jr., to Memphis where he was assassinated.
April 16.
The United States Department of Justice reported that 46
persons had been killed in the rioting that followed the as-
sassination of Martin Luther King, Jr. April 23.
Rev. Ralph D. Abernathy led a "delegation of 100" representatives of minority groups in conferences in Washington,
D.C. with Cabinet members and Congressional leaders and
presented a list of legislative demands for the poor people
of America. April 29.
"Resurrection City," symbol of the Poor People's March on
Washington, D.C., was dedicated, May 13.
In three unanimous decisions the United States Supreme Court
ruled that "freedom of choice" desegregation plans in the
South were inadequate if they did not bring about integration
as well as other plans would. Allowing children of all
races to choose their schools, a plan practiced in 9 out of
10 Southern communities, tended to perpetuate segregation,
declared the Court. May 27.
In a land-mark decision, the United States Supreme Court
ruled that racial discrimination was prohibited in all sales
and rentals of residential and other property. June 18.
The Fourth Assembly of the World Council of Churches,
meeting in Uppsala, Sweden, elected three American blacks
to the Central Committee, the body that makes policy between Assemblies. July 18.
N. Y. Times survey of civil rights movement found lack of
meaningful progress for blacks had led to ferment in movement and changes in groupings and goals among such groups

as the National Association for the Advancement of Colored
People, Congress of Racial Equality, and National Urban
League. July 21.

Arthur Ashe became the first American since 1955 to win
the United States amateur tennis singles title at the Long-
wood Cricket Club in Brooline, Mass. Aug. 25.

The Democratic Party Convention had 337 black delegates --
189 voting, 148 alternates. A Black caucus was convened
several times during the convention under the leadership of
Rep. John Conyers, Jr. (Michigan) and Mayor Richard G.
Hatcher of Gary, Indiana. Aug. 27.

The Rev. Channing E. Phillips of Washington, D.C. was the
first Black ever placed in nomination for President of the
United States at a major party convention at the Democratic
Convention in Chicago. Aug. 28.

Among the resolutions adopted by the 3rd Black Power Conference held in Philadelphia were proposals supporting the
organization of a national Black party for "Progressive and
radical social change." The Rev. Dr. Nathan Wright was
Chairman. Sept. 1.

Arthur Ashe was the first winner of the new United States
Open Championship in tennis at Forest Hills Stadium in
New York City. Sept. 9.

Attorney General of the United States, Ramsey Clark, announced that there was a drop in the number and severity
of riots and disorders in the summer of 1968 compared with
data of former years. Clark noted, however, that riots
following the death of Martin Luther King, Jr. "made April,
1968, the second worst month in recent years." Oct. 3.

James Earl Jones was hailed as the Broadway theater's new-
est "star" after the opening of The Great White Hope. Oct.
5.

Two Black athletes, sprinters Tommie Smith and John Carlos,
used the victory ceremony of the 200-meter dash at the Games
of the 19th Olympiad in Mexico City as a vehicle for a Black
Power demonstration (Smith had won a gold medal for the
event, Carlos a bronze medal for third place). Oct. 16.

Nine Blacks -- a record -- all Democrats, were elected to
the House of Representatives. Nov. 5.

Mrs. Shirley Chisholm defeated James L. Farmer in the
Congressional race in the Bedford-Stuyvesant section of
Brooklyn, N.Y. to become the first Black woman elected to
the House of Representatives. Nov. 5.

Yale University, following a recommendation made by a
faculty-student committee including four student members
of the University's Black Student Alliance, announced that

it would offer a B.A. degree in Afro-American studies. Dec. 12.

1969
The House of Representatives voted to seat Adam Clayton Powell, Congressman from Harlem, fine him $25,000 for alleged mis-use of payroll, and travel funds, and strip him of his 22 years of seniority. Jan. 1.

Charlie Gifford of Charlotte, North Carolina, won the $100,000 Los Angeles Open for $20,000. Gifford was the second man to win a major pro golf tournament. Jan. 12.

U.S. Attorney General Ramsey Clark reported that since the passage of the 1965 Voting Rights Act, voter registration in Alabama, Georgia, Louisiana, and South Carolina had increased from 730,000 to nearly 1,500,000. Jan. 13.

Eldridge Cleaver, a Panther leader sought by the police as a parole violator since November, 1968, remained in hiding as he was inaugurated in absentia in Toronto, Canada, as "president-elect-in-exile" of the United States. Jan. 20.

Roy Campanella was elected to baseball's Hall of Fame by the Baseball Writers Association of America. He is the second Black player to be admitted to the Hall. Jan. 21.

A Black man was appointed to Virginia's State Board of Education for the first time in the State's history when Governor Mills E. Godwin, Jr. appointed Hilary H. Jones to this position. Feb. 1.

James Earl Ray, who pleaded guilty in a Memphis court to murdering Dr. Martin Luther King, Jr., last year, was sentenced to 99 years in prison. March 10.

Former N.Y. Yankee Hector Lopez was appointed manager of the Washington Senators' Buffalo triple A team of the International League. He became the first Black manager in professional baseball. March 20.

A strike of hospital workers -- mostly Black women -- started in Charleston, North Carolina, and turned into a major civil rights movement led by the Southern Christian Leadership Conference. March 20.

The widow of Marine Sgt. Rodney M. Davis, of Macon, Georgia, received the Medal of Honor from Vice-President Spiro Agnew. Davis was killed in 1967, and he was the 10th Black man to receive the award for heroism in Vietnam and the 47th in military history. March 26.

Memorial services for Martin Luther King, Jr. were held throughout the nation. April 4.

The Department of Justice filed its first discrimination suit against a major Southern textile company, charging Cannon Mills with bias in both employment and the rental

of company housing. It marked the first time the government has moved against segregated company-owned housing.
April 8.

Clifford L. Alexander, Jr., resigned as chairman of the
Equal Employment Opportunity Commission, giving as reason
"a crippling lack of administration support." Mr. Alexander
is a Black. April 9.

About 100 Black students seized the Student Union building at
Cornell University. They emerged the next day carrying
17 rifles and shot guns. April 19.

In South Carolina the Rev. Ralph D. Abernath, successor to
Dr. Martin Luther King, Jr., as head of the Southern Christian Leadership Conference, led a march of more than 700
striking Charleston hospital workers. April 22.

The Department of Health, Education, and Welfare told
Antioch College that it might operate an all-Black Black
Studies section as long as nonblacks were not excluded because of race, color, or national origin. But white students
could be excluded on the ground that their background was
not "relevant" to the courses. May 2.

James Foreman, director of the National Black Economic
Development Conference, demanded that churches and
synagogues pay $5,000,000 as reparations to the Black
people. May 2.

Howard Lee was elected the first Black mayor of the predominantly (80%) white city of Chapel Hill, North Carolina. May
6.

Black civil rights leader Charles Evers defeated a white in-
cumbent to become mayor of Fayette, Mississippi. May 13.

In a historic ruling the U.S. Supreme Court decided that the
House of Representatives violated the Constitution in excluding Harlem Representative Adam Clayton Powell from
his seat in the 90th Congress. June 16.

The head of the National Education Association (NEA) Compliance Committee reported that "all but the last step" had
been taken to integrate all NEA state affiliates. NEA is the
country's largest professional organization. July 2.

The Washington Square United Methodist Church in New
York City became the first predominantly white religious
organization to give money to the National Black Economic
Development Conference by handing the group's chief spokesman, James Foreman, a check for $15,000. July 6.

The Department of Justice intensified its school desegregation efforts by accusing the board of education of Chicago
and the state board in Georgia of segregation. The Department contended that Chicago practiced faculty segregation

and that Georgia maintained an unconstitutional dual system.
July 9.
The strike of nonprofessional hospital workers in Charleston ended after 113 days, having brought organized labor and the civil rights movement together for the first time.
July 18.
Presidents of 31 Black colleges ended a 3-day meeting in Mobile, Alabama, by passing a resolution that criticized the federal government's lack of understanding of the role of the 113 predominantly Black colleges in the United States.
July 18.
Columbia University announced the election of the first two Blacks to its Board of Trustees, Franklin A. Thomas and Dr. M. M. Weston. July 25.
In a special election held in Greene County, Alabama, Blacks won four of five seats on the county commission and two seats on the five-member school board, which already included one Black. The victory was hailed by the Rev. Ralph D. Abernathy as "the most significant achievement by Black men since the Emancipation Proclamation." July 29.
The defense attorney for Bobby Seale, the Black Panther party's national chairman held in $25,000 bail on charges involving the murder last May of a former Black Panther in Connecticut, accused the Justice Department of initiating a national campaign to harass the party. Aug. 20.
After hearing that political pressures prompted the government to call for a delay in Mississippi school integration, about half of the staff of lawyers in the Justice Department's Civil Rights Division agreed to protest the Nixon Administration's handling of desegregation policies.
Aug. 27.
The Episcopal Church's House of Delegates voted to grant James Foreman's Black Economic Development Conference $200,000. The organization had demanded the sum as "reparations." Sept. 3.
Josh White, Black blues and folk singer, died. Sept. 5.
Alabama ended its first week of widespread school integration with no trouble and no resistance from white parents although Governor George Wallace had urged defiance by white parents. Sept. 6.
The U.S. Commission on Civil Rights unanimously charged that the Nixon administration has chosen the wrong school desegregation policy and has made that policy an apparent "major retreat." Sept. 12.

Rex Ingram, veteran Black actor whose career spanned 50
years on Broadway and in films, died. He was best known
for his role "De Lawd" in the all-Black 1936 film, The Green
Pastures. Sept. 20
The "Philadelphia Plan", which sets minority hiring guidelines for six skilled construction crafts, was ordered into
effect by Labor Secretary George P. Shultz on federally assisted projects in Philadelphia. Sept. 23.
The first Black mayor of a major American city, Carl. B.
Stokes of Cleveland, won renomination as the Democratic
mayorality candidate. In the primary, he defeated his opponent with a greater percentage of votes than he had in the
1967 primary. Sept. 30.
Senator Edward W. Brooke of Massachusetts became the first
Senator to ask publicly that President Nixon withdraw the
nomination of Clement F. Haynsworth, Jr., to the U.S.
Supreme Court.
Dr. Clifton Reginald Wharton, Jr., was appointed President
of Michigan State University. Dr. Wharton, an economist
from New York City, became the first Black to head a major
public and predominantly white university. Oct. 17.
In a unanimous decision that was a setback for the Nixon
administration, the Supreme Court ordered an end to all
school segregation "at once." In the case of 33 Mississippi
school districts, the court's decision replaced the Warren
court's doctrine of "all deliberate speed" and dismissed the
contention that providing a continuing education should take
precedence over enforcing social justice. Oct. 29.
Democratic Mayor Carl B. Stokes, the first Black to be
major of a major American city, won reelection in a close
race against his Republican opponent. Nov. 4.
Thirty Mississippi school districts were ordered by a federal appeals court to desegregate by December 31 and to
use, with some exceptions, federal integration plans. Nov.
6.
The U.S. Senate rejected the nomination of Clement F.
Haynsworth, Jr., of South Carolina to the U.S. Supreme
Court. Nov. 21.
Police killed Fred Hampton, the Illinois chairman of the
Black Panther party, and another Panther leader with a hail
of shotgun and pistol fire during a raid on an apartment
near the group's headquarters in Chicago. Dec. 4.

1970   James Edwards, Black actor best known for his performance
in the 1949 film, Home of the Brave, died in San Diego,
California, after a heart attack. Jan. 4.

Four Southern governors (Governors Lester Maddox of
Georgia, John J. McKethen of Louisiana, Albert P. Brewer
of Alabama, and Claude R. Kirk of Florida) vowed to defy
the federal government's plan to implement student busing
arrangements in their home states to achieve desegregated
school systems. Jan. 10.
William B. Robertson, a public school supervisor, was appointed by Governor Linwood Holton of Virginia, as a key
member of his executive staff. This is the first time that
a Black served in a Virginia governor's office. Jan. 13.
Integration of school districts in six Deep South States must
take place no later than Feb. 1, the Supreme Court ruled.
This decision overturned a court appeals ruling allowing a
delay until next fall. Jan. 14.
Some cities closed their schools, some governors declared
a special day, and many churches held services on the 41st
anniversary of the birth of Dr. Martin Luther King, Jr.,
the murdered civil rights leader. Jan. 15.
President Nixon nominated Judge G. Harrold Carswell of
Florida to the U.S. Supreme Court. Carswell is regarded
as a racist and conservative. Jan. 19.
The killing of two Black Panthers, one of whom was Fred
Hampton, a 21-year-old leader of the party's Illinois chapter,
in a predawn police raid in Chicago last December was ruled
"justifiable" by a special coroner's jury. Jan. 21.
The National Institute of National Health presented a study
on civil disorders which showed that armed white civilians
were more widely involved in civil disorders during the
last decade than were Blacks. The report was entitled,
A Study of Arrest Patterns in the 1960's Riots. Jan. 22.
Col. Daniel Jones Jr., a fighter-pilot who served as commander of U.S. Forces at Wheelers Air Base in Lybia, was
nominated for rank of brigadier general. Lieut. General
Benjamin O. Davis, Jr., the only other Black general officer
in the Air Force, has retired at the same time. Jan. 25.
Seven Black Panthers who survived a police raid last December 4 were indicted on Chicago on attempted murder charges.
Jan. 30.
Joseph L. Searles 3d was the first Black man to be proposed
for membership on the New York Stock Exchange. Jan. 30.
The deadlines set by federal courts for midterm school
integration passed with small impact on the South, as many
public school officials ignored the orders or closed their
systems temporarily to await further legal development.
Feb. 2.
The Senate and the House approved education appropriation

bills containing amendments introduced by Southern opponents
of school desegregation. The House bill contained three
antibusing and "freedom of choice" amendments designed to
restrict federal power to enforce desegregation. The Senate
bill contained an amendment which would halt busing of
children to achieve racial balance. Feb. 19.

An all-white federal jury acquitted three white Detroit policemen and a Black private guard of conspiring to violate the
civil rights of 10 persons in the Algiers Motel, Detroit, in
1967, where three Blacks were found dead. The prosecution
charged the men with use of excessive force to obtain information about sniping during the Detroit riots. Feb. 25.

School buses bringing Black children to a newly integrated
school in Lamar, South Carolina, were attacked with ax
handles and baseball bats by a mob of raging whites. State
policemen used tear gas and clubs to drive the whites back.
Several children were injured. After the children left, the
mob overturned two of the three buses before being dispersed.
March 3.

William Warfield, the world-famous singer, celebrated his
20th anniversary debut in New York City concert halls at a
recital at Tully Hall in Lincoln Center. March 23.

President Nixon pledged to eliminate officially imposed
segregation in Southern schools but said that until he has
further court guidance he could not require the elimination
of segregation caused by residential patterns. He did,
however, announce plans to allocate $1.5 billion to help
local schools overcome the effects of residentially caused
segregation. March 24.

In an effort to head off a Supreme Court-backed school
integration plan, Governor Claude R. Kirk, Jr., of Florida
ordered Manatee County pupils to ignore the desegregation
order. Kirk also personally assumed control of the county's
school system after suspending the school superintendent.
April 6.

The U.S. Senate refused to confirm the nomination of Judge
G. Harrold Carswell to the Supreme Court in a vote of 51
to 45. April 8.

Governor Kirk of Florida yielded to the authority of a federal court, and announced that he would reinstate the Manatee County school board and direct it to put into effect a
court-ordered-integration plan. The court had ordered
the governor to pay a $10,000-a-day fine unless he released
control of the system. April 12.

Kingman Brewster, Jr., president of Yale University, stated
that in his personal opinion that he was "skeptical" as to

whether Black revolutionaries could get "a fair trial anywhere
in the United States." He said that he was "appalled and
ashamed" that such a situation can exist and blamed police
action against Black Panthers for it. April 24.
Allison Davis was appointed as John Dewey Distinguished
Professor of Education at the University of Chicago, the
first Black man to hold a major endowed chair in this or any
of the great universities in the United States. April 27.
James H. Hubert, the first executive director of the New
York Urban League, died. May 1.
The criminal charges against seven Black Panthers who
survived a Chicago police raid in December 1969 in which
two Black Panthers were killed were dropped after the prosecution said that there was insufficient evidence that any of
the defendants had fired at the police. May 8.
A dusk-to-dawn curfew was imposed on Atlanta, Georgia,
after a night of rioting that left six Blacks dead from police
fire and at least 75 persons injured. Twelve hundred National Guardsmen surrounded the devastated neighborhood.
Governor Lester G. Maddox ordered the Guard to shoot to
kill and called the riot a "Communist conspiracy." May 12.
A student at Jackson (Mississippi) State College and a local
high school senior, both Blacks, were killed in a barrage of
police gunfire that riddled a student dormitory. May 14.
The NAACP gave $50,000 to save a commission set up last
December for a national study of clashes between the police
and the Black Panthers. May 14.
George C. Wallace was elected again as governor of Alabama in a campaign based upon his historical racism. June 2.
Earl Grant, entertainer and organist who was best known
for his instrumental version of "Ebb Tide," died in an automobile crash. June 11.
Federal Judge A. Leon Higginbotham, Jr., was elected a
trustee of Yale University, the first Black person to be
chosen for the institution's governing board since Yale was
founded in 1701. June 15.
Kenneth A. Gibson was elected Mayor of Newark, New Jersey,
thus becoming the first Black man to be elected Mayor of
a major eastern seabord city. June 16.
Officials of the National Education Association testified before a Senate Committee that 5,000 Black teachers and
principals in Southern schools had either been dismissed
or demoted as a result of desegregation. June 16.
The Rev. Henry Jogner, Jr. became the minister of the
Cavalry Methodist Church in Atlanta, Georgia, the first
Black minister to take the pulpit of an all-white Southern

parish of the United Methodist Church, a Protestant giant
in the "Bible Belt." June 26.
The head of the NAACP, Bishop Stephen G. Spottswood, denounced the Nixon administration as anti-Black in its policies.
June 30.
Dr. Felton G. Clark, retired president of Southern University, one of the nation's leading Black educators and a controversial figure in early efforts to integrate lunch counters
in Louisiana, died. July 1.
"It's the job of Congress or the courts" to change the legal
requirements for school integration if the current laws are
insufficient, stated the civil rights chief of the Justice Department before a Senate committee in a defense of administration policy. Democratic members of the committee had
attacked the administration's desegregation policy as being
a set of narrow legalisms. July 13.
Louis E. Lomax, a nationally known Black writer and member of the faculty of Hofstra University in Long Island, N.Y.,
was killed in an automobile crash. He was known as one of
the major interpreters of the integration movement. Aug. 1.
Arrangements were made for graveside services for a Black
soldier killed in Vietnam after a federal judge ordered a
segregated cemetery in Fort Pierce, Florida, to accept the
body. A 72-year-old whitewoman had donated the grave
despite a charter assuring burial only to white plot owners.
Aug. 27.
There was no reported violence as most Southern children
returned to school, many to newly integrated classrooms.
Aug. 31.
Dr. Hugh S. Scott was appointed Superintendent of Schools
by the District of Columbia Board of Education. He became
the first Black school superintendent of a major American
city. Sept. 1.
The killing of two Black students at Jackson State College
the past May was "unreasonable unjustified overreaction"
on the part of Mississippi policemen, reported the President's Commission on Campus Unrest. Oct. 1.
Dr. Ralph J. Bunche, Under Secretary of the United Nations,
received the 8th Annual Family of Man Awards for excellence
from the Council of Churches of the city of New York. Oct.
22.
Wilson Riles defeated Superintendent of Public Instruction
Max Rafferty in one of the most stunning upsets in California political history to become the first Black man ever to
hold statewide office in California. Nov. 4.
A record number of Blacks were elected to the U.S. House

of Representatives. The members elected for the first time were: George W. Collins (Illinois), Ronald V. Dellums (California), Ralph Metcalfe (Illinois), Parren J. Mitchell (Maryland), Charles B. Rangle (New York). All the Representatives were Democrats. Nov. 4.
City Councilman Louis Mason Jr. became the first Black man elected President of Pittsburgh's City Council. Dec. 14.
The Federal Reserve Bank of New York announced the appointment of Whitney Young Jr., Executive Director of the National Urban League, to a three-year term as a Class C director of the bank. He will be the first Black to serve on the bank's board, although Blacks are serving on the boards of other regional banks. Dec. 29.

1971   Dr. Melvin H. Evans, a Black physician, was installed as the first elected Governor of the Virgin Islands. Jan. 4.
Dr. Leon Howard Sullivan, a Black minister from Philadelphia, was elected to the Board of Directors of the General Motors Corporation. He is the first Black to be appointed to one of the world's largest industrial companies. Jan. 4.
Milton B. Allen became Chief Prosecutor of Baltimore, Maryland, the first Black to hold that office in the United States. Jan. 5.
U.S. Black Congressmen boycotted President Richard M. Nixon's State of the Union message because of his "consistent refusal" to listen and respond to the needs and concerns of Blacks in America. Jan. 22.
The U.S. Navy announced that it would name a destroyer escort in honor of Ensign Jesse Leroy Brown, the first Black American aviator and the first naval officer of his race killed in the Korean War. Feb. 22.
The U.S. Census Bureau reported that 1970 statistics indicate that the rate of Black migration from the South to the North has remained steady over the last two decades. March 3.
In the richest single sports event in world history, Joe Frazier won a 15-round decision against challenger Muhammad Ali. March 23.
President Richard M. Nixon accepted the Congressional Black Caucus's list of recommendations dealing with the main problems of American Blacks. He appointed a White House staff panel to study the list. March 25.
Adam Clayton Powell Jr., former Congressman from Harlem, announced his resignation as pastor of the Abyssinian Baptist Church, a post he had held since his father retired in 1937. He indicated he that he would move his permanent residence to Bimini in the Bahamas. April 11.

Samuel Lee Gravely Jr. was promoted to Admiral, thereby
being the first Black Admiral in the history of the U.S.
Navy. April 15.

Vernon E. Jordan, Jr., former Executive Director of the
United Negro Fund, was appointed Executive Director of
the National Urban League, succeeding Whitney M. Young,
Jr. June 15.

The NAACP bestowed the Spingarn Medal upon Dr. Leon
Sullivan, "clergyman, activist and prophet in admiration
of the singular steadfastness with which he had melded religious leadership and social vision for the advancement of
black folk." July 7.

Louis Armstrong, "King of Jazz," died. July 7.

George W. Crockett Jr. of Detroit was elected head of the
Judicial Council, the first formal organization of Black
judges in the United States. Aug. 7.

Ralph Bunche, Undersecretary of the United Nations, died.

Althea Gibson Darden, former winner of the U.S. and Wim-
bledon championships, was elected to the National Lawn
Tennis Hall of Fame in Newport, Rhode Island. Aug. 21.

A federal court judge in Detroit, Michigan, found the Detroit public school system guilty of planned segregation.
Sept. 27.

The Ford Foundation announced that it would award $100
million to private Black colleges over a six-year period to
help them improve their academic and fiscal condition.
Oct. 9.

Mayor Richard G. Hatcher of Gary, Indiana, won re-election to a second term. Nov. 2.

Congressman Charles C. Diggs Jr. (D. Mich.) resigned
from the U.S. delegation to the United Nations to protest
the policies of the Nixon administration dealing with African
nations. He was the first member of an American delegation to resign in protest against U.S. policies. Nov. 17.

1972   A federal court removed the special tax status and concomitant tax benefits granted to fraternal organizations that
exclude Blacks from membership. The ruling came in a suit
brought against Secretary of Treasury John B. Connally and
other government officials by a Black man, C.V. McGolten,
who was denied membership in the Benevolent and Protective
Order of the Elks in Portland, Oregon, because of his race.
Jan. 11.

The Department of Health, Welfare and Education reported
that integration in the South had led to a smaller proportion

of Black students attending totally segregated schools in the South than in other sections of the country. Jan. 12.

Rep. Shirley Chisholm (D. N. Y.) announced that she would seriously seek the Democratic nomination for President of the United States. She was the first Black woman to do so. Jan. 25.

Wilt Chamberlain of the Los Angeles Lakers became the N.B.A.'s all-time rebound champion by getting his 21,772nd rebound in a game against Portland. Jan. 30.

Huey P. Newton, cofounder of the Black Panther Party, announced that the party had given up the "pick up the gun" approach in favor of community work and voter registration. Jan. 30.

The Congressional Black Caucus elected Congressman Stokes (D. Ohio) Chairman, succeeding Charles C. Diggs, Jr. (D. Mich.) who had led the group since its formation as an informal study group in 1969. Feb. 8.

Kerry Pourciau was elected the first Black student president of Louisiana State University. March 7.

Benjamin L. Hooks, Black Memphis attorney and Baptist minister, was named by President Richard M. Nixon to the Federal Communications Commission thereby being the first Black to serve on the commission. April 11.

Adam Clayton Powell, Jr., minister, former Congressman, and protest leader, died. April 4.

Robert Wedgeworth was named Director of the American Library Association, the first Black to head this major organization. April 24.

Major General Frederick E. Davidson, the highest ranking Black officer in the U.S. Army, was assigned to command the 8th Infantry Division in Europe and became the first Black officer to lead an army division. April 25.

Texas State Senator Barbara Jordan won the Democratic primary election in Houston district, defeating three male opponents. May 6.

Angela Davis was acquitted of murder, kidnapping and conspiracy by an all-white jury. The charges grew out of a 1970 shoot-out in which four persons were killed. June 4.

Frank Willis, a Black security guard, summoned police to the Washington, D.C., Watergate complex where five men were arrested for breaking into the offices of the National Democratic Committee. The men carried cameras and surveillance equipment. June 17.

The U.S. Census Bureau reported that the median income for Black families was $6,440 while that for all U.S. families was $10,275, and $10,670 for white families. June 17.

The U.S. Supreme Court rendered its first nonunanimous decision in the field of school desegregation when it ruled, 5-4, that the town of Emporia, Virginia, could not, within the framework of the Constitution, remove its schools from the Greensville County school system, which had a large proportion of Black students. June 22.

U.S. Government officials revealed that Blacks were used as guinea pigs in syphilis experiments at Tuskegee Institute and that doctors had permitted 400 of these patients to go untreated for 40 years. The study was made to determine from autopsies what untreated syphilis did to the human body. June 25.

The U.S. Senate confirmed the appointment of W. Beverly Carter as Ambassador to the Republic of Tanzania. June 26.

The NAACP reported that more school segregation took place in 1971 than in any year since the 1954 Supreme Court decision of <u>Brown</u> v. <u>Board</u> <u>of</u> <u>Education</u>. June 29.

Daniel (Chippie) James, Jr. was promoted to Major General, thereby becoming the highest ranking Black officer in the Air Force. June 29.

The U.S. Dept. of Housing & Urban Development (HUD) Secretary George Romney announced that Floyd McKissick's new town, Soul City, North Carolina, would have $14 million in land development bonds guaranteed by HUD. Soul City would be the first federally guaranteed plan with a Black sponsor and the first outside a metropolitan region. July 3.

Art Williams became the first Black umpire in the National League and officiated in the Los Angeles Dodgers-San Diego Padres game in San Diego. Sept. 22.

Secretary of the Army Robert F. Froehike ordered the clearing of the military records of the 167 "Brownsville Raid" soldiers who were dishonorably discharged by President Theodore Roosevelt in one of the most racist actions ever carried out by an American President. Sept. 28.

The Black National Assembly met in Chicago and established itself as a permanent organizational structure. Rep. Charles C. Diggs, Jr. (D. Mich.) was chosen president, and Mayor Richard G. Hatcher of Gary, Indiana, was voted chairman of the 54-member National Political Council. Oct. 21.

Gordon Parks, photographer, writer, filmmaker, and composer, received the Spingarn Medal for his multifacted creative achievements.

"Jackie" R. Robinson, the first Black to play in major league baseball with the Brooklyn Dodgers, died. Oct. 24.

Barbara Jordan was elected to the House of Representatives as a Democrat from Texas's 18th District. They were the

first Blacks elected to the House from the South since the
turn of the century. Nov. 7.
Theodore Berry was elected first Black mayor of Cincinnati,
Ohio. Dec. 1.
George W. Collins (D. Ill.) was killed in a Chicago airplane
crash. Dec. 8.

1973   Only 52% of Black eligible voters participated in the 1972
             presidential election, according to the U.S. Census Bureau.
             Nationally, 62% of the voting population participated. Jan. 8.
             The U.S. Supreme Court ruled unanimously that a defendant
             had the right to demand that potential jurors be questioned
             about possible racial prejudice. Jan. 17.
             Stanley Scott was appointed the President's liason with mi-
             nority groups, making him the highest-ranking Black in the
             Nixon Administration. Feb. 5.
             The Michigan Department of Health said that the average
             life expectancy for Black males in the state dropped from
             64 to 61.1 years between 1960 and 1970, while the rate for
             whites and for Black women were rising. An official attri-
             buted the decline in part to a rise in homicides, where 70%
             of murder victims were Black males, and to a concentration
             of Black men in physically taxing or dangerous jobs. Feb. 5.
             In a report on marital status based on the 1970 census, the
             Census Bureau reported that the number of intact marriages
             between Blacks and whites were a4,789 in 1970, compared
             to only 51,409 in 1960. All of the net increase was accounted
             for by marriages between Black men and white women.
             Feb. 13.
             The American Federation of Teachers presented its first
             Civil Rights Award to Roy Wilkins, Executive Director of
             the NAACP. Feb. 27.
             The National Black Assembly met in Detroit and set up the
             first practical programs aimed at the group's objective of
             greater Black political power. March 3.
             H.R. Crawford was named Assistant Secretary of Housing
             and Urban Development (HUD) thereby becoming the highest
             ranking Black in the Nixon Administration. March 8.
             The number of Blacks holding the rank of Admiral or Gen-
             eral in the U.S. armed service rose to 16 with the promo-
             tion of three Black Colonels, Charles C. Rogers, Fred C.
             Sheffy, and Roscoe Robinson, to the rank of Brigadier Gen-
             eral. May 23.
             Thomas Bradley was elected Mayor of Los Angeles in a non-
             partisan election, winning against Sam Yorty who was seek-
             ing a fourth term. He was the city's first Black mayor.

Los Angeles's Black population was about 15-18 percent of
the total population. May 29.

Claud W.B. Holman, 69, one of Chicago's most powerful
politicians, a staunch supporter of Mayor Richard Daley,
and president pro tempore of the City Council, died. June 1.

Arna Bontemps, 70, Black poet, author and critic, a leader
of the 1920s movement known as "Harlem Renaissance,"
died. June 4.

Mrs. Cardess R. Collins was elected the first Black woman
to serve in Congress. She was elected as a Democrat to
succeed her husband who was killed in an airplane crash in
his home state of Illinois. June 5.

The Little Rock, Arkansas, school board ratified a final
agreement with the black plaintiffs in the 16-year-old integration suit that had touched off controversy leading to the
dispatch of federal troops to guard Black students entering
the city's Central High School. June 29.

The Rev. Ralph D. Abernathy announced in Atlanta that he
was resigning as president of the Southern Cristian Leadership Conference, effective August 16, when a successor
would be chosen at the organization's annual convention.
July 9.

Delegates to the national convention of the Order of the
Elks voted to rescind the organization's 105-year-old rule
restricting membership to whites. July 19.

The National Black Network, the nation's first Black-owned
and operated news network, began operations with hourly
news feeds to 40 affiliated stations. The network, based in
New York City, was scheduled to provide new reports of interest to Black listeners daily. July 20.

Dr. George A. Wiley, 42, leader of the National Welfare
Rights Organization, who sparked radical reform in welfare
system, and served as coordinator for the Movement for
Economic Justice, died. Aug. 8.

Governor Daniel Walker of Illinois signed a bill legalizing
January 15 as a holiday in honor of the birth date of Dr.
Martin Luther King, Jr. Illinois was the first state to take
this action. Sept. 17.

Diana Sands, 39, a Black actress, won acclaim for her performance on the stage and screen in A Raisin in the Sun
(1959). Sept. 22.

Wilson C. Riles, Superintendent of Public Instruction in
California, was awarded the Spingarn Medal for his outstanding contributions in the field of education.

Clarence Lighter was elected the first Black mayor of Raleigh, North Carolina. Raleigh is only 10 percent Black.
Nov. 6.

1974   The U.S. Bureau of Labor Statistics reported that 166,000 Blacks moved from the Southern states to the North, and 247,000 returned to the South from the North. Jan. 2.

It was reported in the N.Y. Times that increasing financial problems and decreasing enrollments were leading to the demise of many Black colleges in the U.S. Jan. 8.

A group of 16 Black mayors and civil rights leaders held a two-hour meeting with Vice President Gerald R. Ford and afterward expressed hope that Blacks would now have a "sympathetic ear" in the Nixon Administration. Jan. 11.

The Voter Education Project, a private organization based in Atlanta, said 363 Blacks had won office in the South in 1973 off-year elections. According to the group's study, 253 victories were in elections for municipal councils and commissions. There were 63 school board victories, 19 new Black mayors, 14 election commissioners, and 2 state legislators. Feb. 4.

It was decided that a portrait of Dr. Martin Luther King, Jr. would hang in the Georgia capital building in Atlanta. A special biracial commission selected by Governor Jimmy Carter recommended three Georgia Blacks for inclusion in the portraint gallery. Henry McNeal Turner, a Methodist bishop who served in the state legislature in the 1880s, and Lucy Lane, who organized schools in Augusta, Georgia, were the two other Blacks whose portraits would be included. Feb. 7.

Named to the Hall of Fame by the Negro Baseball Selection Committee was James ("Cool Papa") Bell, a renowned base stealer and hitter, whose 26-year career was spent in the Negro Leagues during the 1920s, 30s, and 40s. Feb. 13.

About 1700 delegates to the second National Black Political Convention met in Little Rock, Arkansas, in an atmosphere of conflict between Black nationalist leaders advocating a separatist approach to political action, and the more conservative leaders who favored operating within the traditional political structure. Feb. 15.

Lee Elder became the first Black pro golfer to qualify for the Masters Tournament when he defeated Peter Oosterhuis of England in a sudden-death playoff to win the Monsanto Open in Pensacola, Florida. April 21.

Governor George C. Wallace won 25 percent of the Black vote in his victorious nomination for a fourth term in Alabama. He stressed "opportunities for all" in his campaign. May 5.

Andrew F. Brimmer, first Black member of the Board of Governors of the Federal Reserve System, resigned to accept a position on the faculty of the Harvard Graduate School in Business Administration. May 14.

The Rev. C. Shelby Rooks was named the first Black president of the predominantly white Chicago Theological Seminary. April 8.

The Rev. Dr. Lawrence W. Bottoms, a minister in Decatur, Georgia, was elected to be the first Black moderator of the Presbyterian church in the United States. Blacks comprise less than 10 percent of the membership of churches in the Southern and border states. June 6.

The Boston National Center of Afro-American Artists received an award of $750,000 from the Ford Foundation, first of its kind to a Black cultural center. June 24.

Vice-President Gerald R. Ford addressed the National Urban League convention, marking the first time that one of the top leaders of the Nixon Administration had addressed a major Black organization, civil rights or otherwise. July 27.

A N.Y. Times survey of New York City Blacks indicated little regret over President Nixon's resignation; it was felt that Nixon was unsympathetic toward Blacks. Aug. 11.

Henry (Hank) Aaron broke Ty Cobb's major league baseball record by playing in his 3,034th game. He also hit 715 home-runs, breaking Babe Ruth's record. Black Athletes Hall of Fame inducted whites Branch Rickey and Jack Twyman for their help to Black athletes. Aug. 23.

A Charles Stewart Mott Foundation study on Blacks and minorities living in Michigan showed that Michigan had more elected Black officials than any other, also showed that minority income, education and professional opportunities were rising faster in Michigan than the national average. Sept. 3.

The Birmingham Times, a Black newspaper, endorsed Governor George C. Wallace for reelection. Oct. 1.

Frank L. Stanley, 69, civil rights leader and publisher of the Louisville Defender for 40 years, died. Oct. 9.

Frank Robinson was named major league's first Black manager by the Cleveland Indians. Oct. 9.

"The Augobiography of Miss Jane Pitman," a drama of a woman born in slavery who survives to see the unfurling of the civil rights movement, won an Emmy as best special program of 1973. Cicely Tyson, who portrayed Jane Pitman, won an Emmy for best actress in a special. Oct.

Simon Gourdine, an attorney, became the highest ranking Black administrator in professional sports when the Board of Governors of the National Basketball Association (NBA) named him Deputy Commissioner. Nov. 7.

Black members of the U.S. House of Representatives increased their number by one in the elections, with all 15 incumbents winning and with an upset victory for Harold E. Ford, Democrat, a 29-year-old state representative, over four-term Republican Dan Kuykendall in the 8th District of Tennessee. Blacks made no gains in the Senate, where the only Black member, Edward W. Brooke (R. Mass.) was re-elected to a second term in 1972. The 15 reelected Black Representatives, all Democrats, were Yvonne Brathwaite Burke (Calif.), Shirley Chisholm (N.Y.), William Clay (Mo.), Cardiss Collins (Ill.), John Conyers, Jr. (Mich.), Ronald V. Dellums (Calif.), Charles C. Diggs, Jr., (Mich.), Augustus F. Hawkins (Calif.), Barbara C. Jordan (Texas), Ralph Metcalfe (Ill.), Parren J. Mitchell (Md.), Robert N. C. Nix (Pa.), Charles B. Rangel (N.Y.), Louis Stokes (Ohio), and Andrew Young (Ga.). Nov. 6.

A federal judge in San Francisco ruled that IQ tests must not be given to Black children in California if the tests did not reflect the children's cultural background. Nov. 27.

Raymond P. Alexander, 76, a figure in the civil rights movement for 50 years and senior Philadelphia judge, died. Nov. 24.

1975   President Ford appointed William T. Coleman, a Philadelphia attorney and specialist in transportation law, to be Transportation Secretary in his Cabinet. He was the second Black to hold a cabinet position in history; the first was Robert C. Weaver, Secretary of Housing and Urban Development during the L.B. Johnson Administration. Jan. 14.

Elijah Muhammed died. Feb. 25.

Leaders of the Nation of Islam proclaimed Wallce D. Muhammed their new leader and messenger. Feb. 26.

Frank Robinson made his debut as major league's first Black manager of the Cleveland Indians. He was also the first manager to play since Hank Bauer did it with the Kansas City Athletics in 1961. April 8.

Josephine Baker, 68, an American singer and dancer who became one of France's great music hall stars, died. April 10.

Dr. Max Yergan, 82, a Black leader and educator who also worked for civil rights in Africa, died. April 11.

Stevie Wonder, blind singer-musician-composer, won four Grammy Awards. April 14.

Dr. Percy L. Julian, 76, research chemist who held more than 130 chemical patents, isolated soya protein, was an early synthesizer of cortisone drugs, and was active in the civil rights movement, died. April 19.

James B. Parsons was named as the first Black Chief Judge

of a federal court. He was appointed to the U.S District
Court in Chicago. April 19.
Kivie Kaplan, 71, President of the NAACP since 1966, died.
May 5.
The U.S. Senate confirmed Lowell W. Perry as a member
and chairman of the Equal Employment Opportunity Com-
mission. May 21.
Jackie (Moms) Mabley, 78, a Black commedienne who worked
in vaudeville, nightclubs, radio and theater, died. May 23.
Jacksonville, Mississippi, opened nine new, racially inte-
grated public swimming pools, 12 years after it had drained
its old pools and closed them rather than desegregate them.
In 1967, after a 4-year legal battle, the U.S. Supreme
Court had ruled that the city had been within its legal rights
to close the pools, as the city had shut them down for whites
as well as for Blacks. June 13.
Joseph W. Hatchett was sworn in as the first Black State
Supreme Court Justice in the Post-Reconstruction South.
Reubin Askew, the Governor of Florida who appointed him,
was present at the ceremony in Tallahassee. Sept. 2.
Violence erupted on the second day of the first court-ordered
busing of Black and white school children between a major
city, Louisville, Kentucky, and its suburb, Jefferson County.
Sept. 7.

A survey conducted by the Council on Municipal Performance
found Chicago, Illinois, to be the most racially segregated
Northern city in the United States. Nov. 9.
John Hope Franklin, historian of the Black's experience in
America, was elected by the National Council on Humanities
to give its 5th annual lecture.

1976   The N.Y. Times reported that over 1,800 Blacks now hold
elective office in the South.
National Institute of Arts & Letters named Gwendolyn
Brooks a member; she is first Black woman to be elected
to the Institute.
Mehary Medical College, the nation's only privately financed
medical college established for Blacks celebrated its 100th
anniversary this year.
Paul Robeson, All-American athlete, scholar, actor, con-
cert artist, global fighter for humanitarian causes, died in
Philadelphia at the age of 76.
The first Black director of the Detroit Public Library, Mrs.
Clara Jones, was installed as the first Black president of
the American Library Association.

Texas Southern University named its law school the Thurgood Marshall School of Law in honor of the nation's first
Black Supreme Court Justice.
Singer Natalie Cole, daughter of Nat "King" Cole, received
two Grammy Awards as the Best Artist of the Year and Best
Female Rhythm and Blues Vocalist.
Federal Communications Commissioner Benjamin L. Hooks
was elected by the NAACP Board to succeed Roy Wilkins as
executive director of the country's oldest and largest Black
organization.
Rev. Dr. Joseph H. Evans of New York was elected presi-
dent of the predominantly white United Church of Christ
and became the first Black president of the denomination.
Mayor Kenneth A. Gibson became the first Black president
in the 43 year history of the Conference of Mayors.
Rear Admiral Samuel L. Gravely was promoted to the rank
of vice-admiral and assigned to command the U.S. Third
Fleet, thereby becoming the first Black commander of a
Navy fleet.
Symphony orchestra conductor Dean Dixon died in Zurich,
Switzerland, at the age of 61.
The National Association of Black Journalists was organized
in Washington, D.C.
Secretary of Agriculture Earl Butz resigned after acknow-
ledging that he had been guilty of "gross indiscretion" when
he made profane and scandalous remarks about Blacks to a
reporter.
Dr. Henry A. Hill was named president of the American
Chemical Society and became the first Black to head the
Society.
Hank Aaron of the Milwaukee Braves retired active base-
ball to become head of the Atlanta Braves' farm system.
The U.S. House of Representatives established a special
committee to investigate the assassinations of John F. Kennedy and Martin Luther King Jr.

1977   President Jimmy Carter named two Blacks to play important
roles in his new Administration: Patricia Harris will serve
in his cabinet as Secretary of Urban Affairs and Housing
Development, and Congressman Andrew E. Young will be
the United States Representative to the United Nations.
Representative Shirley Chisholm of Brooklyn, N.Y. became
the second woman in memory and the first Black woman ever
named to a seat on the influential House Rules Committee.

APPENDICES

SELECTED BIBLIOGRAPHY OF THE AFRO-AMERICAN

Adams, Russel L., Great Negroes Past and Present, 3rd ed., Chicago: Afro-Am Publishing Co., 1970.

Adler, Mortimer J., and Van Doren, Charles, editors, The Negro in American History, Chicago: Encyclopedia Britannica Education Co., 1969

Aptheker, Herbert, A Documentary History of the Negro People in the United States, New York: The Citadel Press, 1968, 2 vols.

Barley, Ronald W., Black Business Enterprise: Historical and Contemporary Perspectives, New York: Basic Books, 1971.

Burt, McKinley, Black Inventors of America, Portland, Oregon: National Book Co., 1969.

Butcher, Margaret Just, The Negro in American Culture, 2d ed., New York: Knopf, 1971.

Dormon, James H., The Afro-American Experience: A Cultural History Through Emancipation, New York: Wiley, 1974.

Foner, Philip S., Organized Labor and the Black Worker, 1619-1973, New York: Praeger Publishing Co., 1973.

_____. Voice of Black America: Major Speeches by Negroes in the United States, 1797-1971, New York: Simon & Schuster, 1972.

Franklin, John Hope, From Slavery to Freedom: A History of the Negroes in America, 4th ed., New York: Knopf, 1974.

Frazier, Edward F., The Negro Church in America, 1894-1962. The Black Church Since Frazier, C. Eric Lincoln, New York: Schoken Books, 1974.

Gayle, Addison, The Way of the New World: The Black Novel in America, New York: Anchor Press, 1975.

Hamilton, Charles V., The Black Experience in American Politics, New York: G.P. Putnam's Sons, 1974.

Harrison-Ross, Phyliss, The Black Child: A Parent's Guide, New York: P.H. Wyden, 1973.

Hatch, James V., Black Image on the American Stage, 1770-1970, New New York: DBS Publications, 1970.

Hughes, Langston, The Poetry of the Negro, 1746-1970, Garden City, N.Y.: Doubleday, 1970.

Journal of Negro History (Published quarterly by the Association for the Study of Negro Life and History, 1538 Ninth Street, N.W., Washington, D.C.)

Katz, William Loren, general editor, The American Negro: His History and Literature, New York: Arno Press, 1968, 45 vols.

Lerner, Gerda, Black Women in White America: A Documentary History, New York: Pantheon Books, 1972.

Miller, Elizabeth W., The Negro in America: A Bibliography, Cambridge: Harvard University Press, 1970, 2nd ed.

Porter, Dorothy B., The Negro in the United States: A Selected Bibliography, Washington, D.C.: Library of Congress, 1970.

Quarles, Benjamin, The Negro in the American Revolution, Chapel Hill: University of North Carolina Press, 1961.

_____., The Negro in the Civil War, Boston: Little, Brown & Co., 1953.

Salk, Erwin A., A Layman's Guide to Negro History, New York: McGraw-Hill, 1967.

Schatz, Walter, editor, Directory of Afro-American Resources, New York: R. R. Bowker Co., 1970.

Welsch, Erwin K., The Negro in the United States: A Research Guide, Bloomington: Indiana University Press, 1966.

Wolseley, Roland E., The Black Press USA, Ames: Iowa State University Press, 1971.

Wolton, Hanes, Study & Analysis of Black Politics: A Bibliography, Metuchen, N.J.: Scarecrow Press, 1974.

HISTORY & LITERATURE COLLECTIONS

1. Tuskegee Institute, Hollis Burke Frissel Library, Washington Collection, Tuskegee, Ala. 11,000 volumes.
2. Philander Smith College Library, 812 W. 13th St., Little Rock, Ark.
3. University of California (Santa Barbara), Wyles Collection, Goleta, Calif. 13,153 volumes. Emphasis primarily on the Negro as a slave, and implications of slavery and the Civil War.
4. Yale University Library, James Weldon Johnson Memorial Collection of Negro Arts and Letters, New Haven, Conn. Manuscripts and pictures.
5. Howard University Library, Negro Collection, Washington, D.C. 70,000 volumes.
6. Paine College, Warren A. Chandler Library, Augusta, Ga. 396 volumes. Shelflist only, especially race problem as it concerned churches in the Old South.
7. Fort Valley State College, Henry Alexander Hunt Memorial Library, Fort Valley, Ga. 861 volumes.
8. Savannah State College Library, Savannah, Ga. 1,000 volumes. Includes pamphlet and clipping file.
9. Johnson Publishing Company Library, 1820 S. Michigan Ave., Chicago, Ill. 2500 volumes. Pictures, photostats, microfilm.
10. Dillard University Library, 2601 Gentilly Blvd., New Orleans, La. Card index on Negroes in New Orleans, from newspapers covering the period 1850-1865.
11. Xavier University Library, Palmetto and Pine St., New Orleans, La. Restricted use, closed August. Manuscripts, maps, pictures, photostats, microfilm.
12. Detroit Public Library, 5201 Woodward, Detroit, Mich. 849 volumes. Includes music, recordings, dance, drama.
13. St. Augustine Seminary Library, Divine Word Seminary, Bay St. Louis, Miss. 500 volumes. Maintained for missionary work among Negroes.
14. Rust College Library, Magee Memorial Library, Holly Springs, Miss. 3,659 volumes. Includes books by Negroes.
15. Tougaloo College, Eastman Library, Tougaloo, Miss.
16. Bronxville Public Library, 201 Pondfield, Bronxville, N.Y. Books presented in honor of Dr. Ralph J. Bunche, for books by and of the Negro.
17. Columbia University Libraries, Special Collections, Alexander Gumby Collection, New York 10027.
18. New York Public Library Branch, Schomburg Collection, 103 W. 135th St., New York 10027. 33,500 volumes. A library of books, periodicals, manuscripts, clippings, pictures, prints, records, and sheet music which attempts to record the entire experience of people of African descent—historical and contemporary. Restricted use: materials must be used on the premises.
19. University of North Carolina, Louis Round Wilson Library, Chapel Hill, N.C.
20. Western Carolina College Library, Cullowhee, N.C.
21. Duke University Library, Durham, N.C.

22. Bennett College, Thomas F. Holgate Library, Greensboro, N.C. 1,481 volumes.
23. Richard B. Harrison Public Library, 214 S. Blount St., Raleigh, N.C. 3,500 volumes. Mimeographed bibliographies available.
24. The Rutherford B. Hayes Library, 1337 Hayes Ave., Fremont, Ohio. 65,000 volumes.
25. Wilberforce University, Carnegie Library, Daniel Alexander Payne Collection, Wilberforce, Ohio. 4,500 volumes. Includes manuscripts and pictures.
26. Lincoln University, Vail Memorial Library, Lincoln University, Penna. 2,900 volumes. Includes African materials.
27. The Free Library of Philadelphia, Social Science and History Department, Negro Collection, Logan Square, Philadelphia, Penna. 900 volumes.
28. Starks Library, Benedict College, Taylor and Harden St., Columbia, S.C. 29204. 28,100 volumes. Includes manuscripts, maps, pictures, slides.
29. Fisk University Library, Erastus Milo Cravath Memorial Library, Nashville, Tenn. 10,000 volumes. Includes manuscript collection. Restricted use: non-circulating.
30. Texas Southern University Library, Heartman Collection, 3201 Wheeler, Houston, Tex. 11,428 volumes. Includes maps and photographs.
31. Hampton Institute, Collis P. Huntington Memorial Library, George Foster Peabody Collection, Hampton, Va. 9,289 volumes.
32. Virginia State College Library, Norfolk Division, 2401 Corprew Ave., Norfolk, Va.
33. Virginia Union University, William J. Clark Library, 1500 Lombardy St., Richmond, Va. 1,650 volumes.

Excerpts From
THREE LANDMARK CIVIL RIGHTS EXECUTIVE ORDERS

1. Executive Order 8802 Reaffirming Policy of Full Participation in the Defense Program by All Persons, Regardless of Race, Creed, Color, or National Origin, and Directing Certain Action in Furtherance of Said Policy.

Whereas it is the policy of the United States to encourage full participation in the national defense program by all citizens of the United States, regardless of race, creed, color, or national origin, in the firm belief that the democratic way of life within the Nation can be defended successfully only with the help and support of all groups within its borders; and

Whereas there is evidence that available and needed workers have been barred from employment in industries engaged in defense production solely because of considerations of race, creed, color, or national origin, to the department of workers' morale and of national unity:

Now, therefore, by virtue of the authority vested in me by the Constitution and the statutes, and as a prerequisite to the successful conduct of our national defense production effort, I do hereby reaffirm the policy of the United States that there shall be no discrimination in the employment of workers in defense industries or government because of race, creed, color, or national origin, and I do hereby declare that it is the duty of employers and of labor organizations, in defense industries, without discrimination because of race, creed, color, or national origin;

And it is hereby ordered as follows:

. . . .

3. There is established in the Office of Production Management a Committee on Fair Employment Practices, which shall consist of a chairman and four other members to be appointed by the President. . . .

June 25, 1941

2. Executive Order 9808 Establishing The President's Committee on Civil Rights.

Whereas the preservation of civil rights guaranteed by the Constitution is essential to domestic tranquility, national security, the general welfare, and the continued existence of our free institutions; and

Whereas the action of individuals who take the law into their own hands and inflict summary punishment and weak personal vengeance is

83

subversive of our democratic system of law enforcement and public criminal justice, and gravely threatens our form of government; and

Whereas it is essential that all possible steps be taken to safeguard
our civil rights:

Now, therefore, by virtue of the authority vested in me as President
of the United States by the Constitution and the statutes of the United States,
it is hereby ordered as follows:

1. There is hereby created a committee to be known as the President's Committee on Civil Rights, which shall be composed of the following-
named members, who shall serve without compensation:
. . . .

2. The Committee is authorized on behalf of the President to inquire
into and to determine whether and in what respect current law-enforcement
measures and the authority and means possessed by Federal, State, and
local governments may be strengthened and improved to safeguard the civil
rights of the people.
. . . .

5. The Committee shall make a report of its studies to the President in writing, and shall in particular make recommendations with respect
to the adoption or establishment, by legislation or otherwise, of more adequate and effective means and procedures for the protection of the civil rights
of the people of the United States.

Harry S. Truman

The White House
December 5, 1946

3. Executive Order 9981 Establishing The President's Committee on equality Of Treatment And Opportunity In the Armed Forces.

Whereas it is essential that there be maintained in the armed services
of the United States the highest standards of democracy, with equality of
treatment and opportunity for all those who serve in our country's defense:

Now, therefore, by virtue of the authority vested in me as President of the United States, by the Constitution and the statutes of the United
States, and as Commander in Chief of the armed services, it is hereby
ordered as follows:

1. It is hereby declared to be the policy of the President that there
shall be equality of treatment and opportunity for all persons in the armed

forces without regard to race, color, religion, or national origin. This policy shall be put into effect as rapidly as possible, having due regard to the time required to effectuate any necessary changes without impairing efficiency or morale.

. . . .

Harry S. Truman

The White House
July 26, 1948

AN OUTLINE OF AFRO-AMERICAN HISTORY

Europeans Colonize the Americas, 1450-1763

I. The role of the Black in Early America

    A. Free, slave, and indentured Negroes on the Spanish, French, Dutch, Portuguese, and British explorations to the New World.
        1. With Pizarro in Peru
        2. With Cortes in Mexico
        3. With Balboa on discovery of the Pacific Ocean
        4. With De Ayllon in Florida
        5. With Coronado in New Mexico
        6. With Certier and Champlain in North America
        7. With the Jesuits in Canada and in the Mississippi Valley
        8. With the French in Louisiana

    B. The Black Explorers
        1. Estavanico ("Little Stephen")
        2. Jean Baptiste Pointe de Sable in Chicago
        3. Nuflio de Olan with Balboa

    C. English, Black, Scotch, Irish, and Herman indentured servants in the New World.

    D. A basis of equality for Blacks from completion of indentureship between 1623-1660 (voted, testified in court, accumulated land, and mingled freely with other people).

    E. A Black slave labor force in the New World.
        1. Rise of Black enslavement due, in part, to failure of making Indians effective slaves.
        2. In parts of Latin America -- mining and agriculture.
        3. In West Indies-- sugar
        4. In Southern colonies-- tobacco, cotton, rice, indigo.

II. The plantation system in the British North American colonies.

    A. Description, development of plantation system.

    B. Causes for growth.

    C. Change from use of indentured servants to slaves.

    D. Life on a plantation for Black slaves.

III. Free Blacks -- in 1790, more than 59,000 free Blacks in the United States, with more than half in the South: farmers, artisans, mechanics, laborers, seafaring men, hatters, shopkeepers, traders, waiters, cooks, hairdressers, domestice servants, and musicians.

Thirteen English Colonies Win Independence, 1763-1783

I. A turning point toward slaves and slavery in some areas.

A. 1755, the Quakers" position against the importation of slaves.

B. Natural rights philosophy vs. slavery

C. Thomas Jefferson's call for the end of all slave trade and slavery in North America (in 1776 he protested because the King did not stop the slave trade).

D. Stoppage of the slave trade in some states and manumission acts in Pennsylvania, Connecticut, New York, Rhode Island, and New Jersey from 1780-1784.

E. Slavery forbidden in the Northwest Territory by the Ordinance of 1787.

II. Black participation in the War for Independence (on both English and American sides).

A. 5,000 Blacks out of 300,000 total American troops.
   1. Crispus Attucks
   2. Salem Poor
   3. Peter Salem
   4. Austin Dabney
   5. Lemuel Haynes
   6. Tack Sisson
   7. Deborah Gannett

B. The escape of 100,000 Blacks from slavery.

Americans Become a Nation, 1783-1823

I. Government leaders' concern with economic and political stability.

A. Compromises
   1. The count of slaves (three-fifths of slaves counted as population for basis of representation).
   2. Article I, Section 9, slave trade, until 1808.

B. Growth of banks, corporations, insurance companies, canals, and turnpikes after 1790; "King Cotton".

C. Powerful pro-slavery interests awakened at this time.

II. Development of slavery in the cotton-growing South due to technological changes in the United States and England.

III. Contributions by intellectual Blacks in early United States

A. Phyllis Wheatley

B. Benjamin Banneker

C. Prince Hall

D. Jupiter Hammon

E. Gustavus Vassa

IV. Unchanged status of Blacks, slave and free, in spite of the Bill of Rights (1791).

A. Uncertainty of full civil liberties to free Blacks.

B. Elimination of three-fifths representation rule and establishment of full citizenship rights to Blacks by Thirteenth and Fifteenth Amendments.

Concern For Human Rights Increases, Yet Slavery Expands, 1823-1860

I. Abolition movement, a part of the Humanitarian trend.

A. Black leaders
    1. Martin R. Delaney
    2. Henry Highland Garnet
    3. William H. Day
    4. Frederick Douglass
    5. Samuel Cornish
    6. Robert Purvis
    7. William Wells Brown
    8. James W.C. Pennington
    9. Harriet Tubman
    10. F. Ellen Watkins
    11. William Cooper Nell

B. White leaders
    1. Elijah P. Lovejoy
    2. Wendell Phillips
    3. Sarah and Angeline Grimke
    4. William Lloyd Garrison
    5. Louis and Arthur Tappan
    6. Theodore Dwight Weld
    7. James G. Birney
    8. Harriet Beecher Stowe
    9. John Greenleaf Whittier

II. Insurrections against slavery.

    A. Gabriel Prosser (Gabriel's Revolt) 1800

    B. Denmark Vesey, 1822

    C. Nat Turner (Turner's Rebellion), 1831

    D. John Brown, 1859

III. Religious groups and leaders in the Humanitarian movement.

    A. Quakers, Methodists, Congregationalists, Baptists
        1. Underground Railroad
        2. Schools for Blacks

    B. Many Black ministers, leaders in the abolition movement
        1. Henry Highland Garnet
        2. James W.C. Pennington
        3. Samuel Cornish

IV. Higher education opportunities for Blacks

    A. Avery College for Negroes in Pittsburg, 1852.

    B. Ashman Institute (later Lincoln University) in Pennsylvania, 1854.

    C. Wilberforce College near Xenia, Ohio, 1856.

    D. John Russworm, first Black graduate from Bowdoin, 1862;
publisher of first Black newspaper, Freedom's Journal.

    E. Admission of Blacks to Oberlin College in 1830.

Technology, Business Enterprise, Westward Expansion, And
Internal Improvements Spur Economic Growth, 1787-1860

I. Industrial East

    A. Increased slavery in the South related to the growth of the
manufacturing of cotton cloth.

    B. Free Blacks, not generally employed as were the immigrant
factory and industrial labor workers.

II. "King Cotton" South

    A. Slave system, different economic pattern from the rest of the nation.

    B. The South, a region united politically, economically, and socially by slavery.

III. Frontier West

    A. Frontiersmen and miners
        1. James P. Beckworth
        2. Jacob Dodson

    B. Homesteaders
        1. George W. Bush (Puget Sound)
        2. Hiram Young (Independence, Missouri)

    C. Movement westward by settlers holding respective sectional attitudes toward slavery.

IV. Black inventors" contributions in this period.

    A. Louis Temple (standard harpoon for whaling industry)

    B. James Forten (device for handling sails)

    C. Henry T. Blair (patented corn harvester)

    D. Herbert Rillieux (patented evaporating pan in sugar refining).

Slavery Splits The Nation; Reconstruction Fails The Black, 1860-1877

I. Threat to Southern political power due to Republican triumph in 1860 election; nation at the brink of war.

II. The Civil War

    A. Emancipation Proclamation of January 1863.
        1. Support gained from people influenced by the abolitionists
        2. European opinion influenced
        3. Stimulated hope among Black slaves; thousands flocked to Union armies

B. The Black in the Civil War
      1. 180,000 in the Army; 29,000 in the Navy; 40,000 Black deaths; 21 Black recipients of the Congressional Medal of Honor (Joachim Pease and John H. Lawson).
      2. Blacks commissioned as officers in the Union Army
      3. Escape of 100,000 slaves from plantations to headquarters around Washington: a Southern loss; Northern gain.

III. Political, social, civil rights" effects resulting from the Reconstruction Period in the South.

    A. Southerners
      1. Solid South
      2. Hatred and denial of Negro suffrage
      3. Black political leaders in postwar South
      4. The "new industrial elite's" political and economic power
      5. Disregard for law and legal procedures; use of violence and force; the rise of the Ku Klux Klan.

    B. The Blacks
      1. Republicans
      2. Loss of faith in local self-government
      3. Looking to national government for protection
      4. Laborers at the bottom of the scale in urban areas
      5. Propertyless
      6. Sharecroppers, sometimes share tenants
      7. Intensively unemployed in urban areas
      8. Shorn of political power

IV. Education for Blacks, a concern of many in the North and in the South, 1860-1900.

    A. Higher education supported by private funds.
      1. George Peabody
      2. John D. Rockefeller
      3. Andrew Carnegie
      4. William Baldwin, Jr.
      5. Robert C. Ogden

    B. Black educational institutions
      1. Fisk
      2. Atlanta
      3. Tougaloo
      4. Hampton
      5. Shaw
      6. Morehouse

7. Biddle
8. Tuskegee (Booker T. Washington)

C. Open door to Black applicants in Northern colleges and universities; 34 institutions of higher learning established.

D. Education for Black children
    1. Freedmen's Bureau, 1865-1870
        (a) 4,239 free schools for Blacks
        (b) 9,307 teachers
        (c) 247,333 pupils
    2. Julius Rosenwald Fund
        (a) 5,357 school buildings
        (b) 663,615 pupils
    3. Education in the new Souther constitutions
    4. George Peabody Fund
        (a) $2,000,000 for public schools for Blacks
        (b) Some money for George Peabody College for teachers, Nashville, Tennessee
    5. Substantial support for education from Blacks themselves: between 1870 to 1899, $70 million in direct and indirect taxes collected for educational purposes
    6. $15 million in tuition and fees paid by Blacks to educational institutions

E. Substandard educational provisions for Black children in the South
    1. 1907-1908, ratio of money spent-- $5.67 for white teachers' salaries; $1 for Black teachers ' salaries
    2. 1929-1930, ratio: of money spent-- $6.46 for white teachers' salaries; $1 for Black teachers" salaries.

The Economy And Democracy Grow, 1865-1917

I. Retrenchment of Black political, social, and economic rights in the South

A. Poll taxes, complicated voting procedures, "grandfather clause," voting disqualifications for Blacks.

B. Black sharecropper and tenant farmer; lack of economic opportunities in factories of New South.

C. Rise of racism and Jim Crowism increase of lynchings; new emphasis on doctrine of white supremacy and Black inferiority.
    1. Movement of anti-Black feeling to North and West
    2. Deep inroads by Ku Klux Klan
    3. 3,000 lynchings between 1882-1900

D. Plessy vs. Ferguson

II. Cheap labor supply for Northern industrial plants and mines up to 1914 by Eastern and Southern European immigrants; no place in industry for Blacks until after the stoppage and restriction of immigrants after 1914.

III. Urbanization of the Black after 1910

    A. From the agrarian, unskilled stage to the lowest rung of industrial unskilled laborers.
        1. Excluded from craft unions and skilled jobs
        2. Remained in severe poverty, crowded ghettos, and in state of constant unemployment.

    B. Between 1988 and 1933 both major political parties, more or less, unconcerned about the economic, political, and social conditions of the Black in the South and in the North.
        1. 1,000,000 Black farmers organized in Colored Farmers Alliance and Co-operative Union because of Populists' call for Black political equality.
        2. South and West reaction to this: intensified white supremacy

IV. Black reaction to retrenchment

    A. Niagara Movement, 1905

    B. NAACP, 1909

    C. National Urban League, 1910

    D. Publications: Boston Guardian, 1901; Chicago Defender, 1905; Crisis, 1910

V. Black inventors

    A. Granville T. Woode (patents for air brakes).

    B. Elijah McCoy (automatic machine lubricator).

    C. Jan E. Matzeliger (shoe laster).

    D. Lewis Latimer (made drawings for Bell's telephone: Maxim gun; carbon filament for the Maxim electric lamp; worked in Edison's laboratory).

    E. John P. Parker (screw for tobacco presses and founder of Ripley Foundry and Machine Company).

F. George Washington Carver (scientist, inventor, and educator).

VI. Rise of Black small businessmen

A. Charles Clinton Spaulding (North Carolina Mutual Life Insurance Company)

B. Some Black banks, grocery stores, drugstores, lumber mills, small construction businesses; beauty culture business (Sarah Spencer, Madam Walker, A.E. Malone).

The Nation Takes A Part In World Affairs, 1865-1930

I. The Black in national defense

A. Black unites organized as part of the regular military establishment
                         1. 9th Cavalry, 1886
                         2. 10th Cavalry , 1866
                         3. 24th Infantry, 1869
                         4. 25th Infantry, 1869

B. Blacks serve in the Spanish-American War

C. 350,000 Blacks in the armed forces in World War I

D. 200,000 Blacks served overseas in World War I, both as combat and noncombat troops.

II. The Black in diplomacy

A. Ebenezer D. Bassett, Minister Resident and Consul General in Haiti, 1869.

B. James M. Turner, Minister Resident and Consul General in Liberia, 1871

C. Henry Highland Garnet, Minister Resident and Consul General in Liberia, 1882.

III. Harlem "Renaissance"

The Nation Suffers Depression And War, 1930-1945

I. The Depression, as it affected the Black

A. The Black, the first to be fired and the last to be hired

B. Unemployment
    1. By 1933 one of every four Blacks on relief
    2. Blacks, 3,000,000 out of 18 million on relief

C. Animosity toward Blacks because of competition for jobs

D. Communist propaganda not effective with Blacks in spite of severe hardships

II. The New Deal

A. The social Security Act of 1935, most significant New Deal measure for Blacks
    1. Old-age benefits to workers
    2. Unemployment insurance
    3. Aid to the blind and crippled
    4. Aid to dependent mothers and children
    5. Aid to destitute old people

B. Low-cost housing activities
    1. Decrease in crowded conditions of Black families
    2. Better housing in more than twenty-five cities

C. The Civilian Conservation Corps' Black enrollment in May of 1935, 16,000

D. Aid to Black farmers
    1. Bankhead-Jones Farm Tenant Act, 1937
    2. Farm Security Administration rehabilitation loans

E. Wagner Labor Relations Act, 1935

    1. Steel, coal, iron, mine, electric, garment, and auto workers in industrial unions
    2. 210,000 Blacks in industrial unions (C.I.O.) in 1940 membership

III. World War II and the Black

A. Wartime focus on Blacks' place in the military and in industry
    1. Uncertainty about Black rights because of discrimination during and after World War I

2. Contradiction over discrimination at home and in the military and over the struggle against Nazi and Fascist racial superiority dogma.

B. End of discrimination in defense industries, 1941

C. Beginning of integration of ground troops, 1945

D. 1,000,000 Black men and women in uniforms, including 6,000 officers

IV. The United Nationa

A. "All human beings are born free and equal in dignity and rights.' (Universal Declaration of Human Rights)

B. Most prominent American Black participants at formation of United Nations, June 1945
1. Ralph Bunche
2. Mary McLeod Bethune
3. W.E.B. DuBois

C. Charter provision of United Nations appealing to Blacks: "Respect for human reights and fundamental freedoms for all without distinction as to race, sex, languages, or religion."

American Deal With Economic Growth, The War On Poverty,
Civil Rights, World Problems, 1946-Present

I. Expanding civil rights

A. Truman's Civil Rights Commission, 1946

B. Truman's executive order integrating armed forces, 1948

C. Brown vs. The Board of Education, 1954
1. A reversal of Plessy vs. Ferguson
2. An outlawing of racial discrimination in the public schools

D. Civil rights laws
1. The Civil Rights Law, 1957
2. The Civil Rights Law, 1960
3. Initiation by Congress of the Twenty-Fourth Amendment, 1962
4. The Civil Rights Act, 1965

II. Southern reaction and violence to progress in civil rights laws

   A. Resistance to civil rights laws
      1. Little, Rock, Arkansas
      2. Montgomery, Alabama
      3. Oxford, Mississippi
      4. Birmingham, Alabama
      5. Philadelphia, Mississippi

   B. Renewed activities by the Ku Klux Klan

   C. Token compliance toward integration in Southern schools
      1. In Southern states, Blacks in school with whites, 1.18%
      2. In border states, Blacks in school with whites, 54.8%

   D. Apathy of Southerners to acts of violence against Blacks

III. In behalf of civil rights

   A. Protestants

   B. Catholics

   C. Jewish organizations

   D. National Association for the Advancement of Colored People,
Roy Wilkins

   E. National Urban League, Whitney M. Young

   F. Student Nonviolent Coordinating Committee, James Forman,
John Lewis, Stokely Carmichael

   G. Congress of Racial Equality, James Farmer, Floyd McKissick

   H. A.F.L.-C.I.O.

   I. Conference of Federated Organizations

   J. Southern Christian Leadership Conference, the Rev. Dr. Martin
Luther King

IV. Nationalists

   A. Black Muslims, Elijah Muhammad

   B. Organization of Afro-American Unity, Malcolm X.

V. Desperation

      A. Percent distribution of white and Black employed by occupational fields, 1910-1970

      B. Income comparison of whites and nonwhites

      C. Political (voting registration in Southern states in 1959 and 1964 indicates some slight improvements)

      D. Social (stereotypes about Blacks false and incriminating; permeate much of the white community; cause discrimination in housing and in educational opportunities)

VI. Black reaction regarding

      A. Riots in Rochester, Philadephia, New York City, Los Angeles, Chicago

      B. Optimism (almost 75% of Blacks questioned replied that they thought white attidtudes toward them would be better in the next five years)

VII. Federal Government's acts of intervention

      A. Federal troops in Little Rock, in University, Alabama

      B. Nationalized Guard in Oxford, Mississippi

      C. Department of Justice, Federal Bureau of Investigation, federal voting registrars

PREDOMINANTLY BLACK COLLEGES & UNIVERSITIES

Four-year, regionally accredited black-dominated
colleges and universities in the United States.

States and Institutions*	Location	Year Founded	Enrollment	Faculty
ALABAMA:				
Alabama A & M University*	Normal	1875	3,009	156
Alabama State*	Montgomery	1874	2,704	115
Miles College	Burmingham	1905	1,270	78
Oakwood College	Huntsville	1896	684	45
Stillman College	Tuscaloosa	1876	660	45
Talladega College	Talladega	1867	520	57
Tuskegee Institute	Tuskegee	1881	3,073	246
ARKANSAS:				
Arkansas Baptist College	Little Rock	1884	430	39
Philander Smith College	Little Rock	1877	670	45
University of Arkansas*	Pine Bluff	1873	2,936	167
DELAWARE:				
Delaware State College*	Dover	1891	1,921	105
DISTRICT OF COLUMBIA:				
District of Columbia Teachers College*		1851	2,878	155
Federal City College*		1966	7,184	300
Howard University		1867	10,152	1,400
FLORIDA:				
Bethune-Cookman College	Daytona Beach	1872	1,219	61
Edward Waters College	Jacksonville	1866	803	50
Florida A & M University*	Tallahassee	1887	4,944	295
Florida Memorial College	Miami	1879	821	50
GEORGIA:				
Albany State College*	Albany	1903	1,926	133
Atlanta University	Atlanta	1865	1,048	--
Clark College	Atlanta	1869	1,182	107
Ft. Valley State College*	Ft. Valley	1939	2,373	114

* Public institution

99

States and Institutions*	Location	Year Founded	Enrollment	Faculty
GEORGIA (cont.):				
Interdenominational Theological Center	Atlanta	1958	164	--
Morehouse College	Atlanta	1867	1,227	84
Morris Brown College	Atlanta	1881	1,524	92
Paine College	Augusta	1882	737	61
Savannah State College*	Savannah	1776	2,728	105
Spelman College	Atlanta	1881	1,118	90
KENTUCKY:				
Kentucky State*	Frankfort	1886	1,970	145
LOUISIANA:				
Dillard University	New Orleans	1869	982	112
Grambling College*	Grambling	1901	3,193	203
Southern University*	Baton Rouge	1880	8,414	534
Southern University*	New Orleans	1956	2,134	--
Xavier University	New Orleans	1925	1,554	131
MARYLAND:				
Bowie State College*	Bowie	1865	2,353	137
Coppin State College*	Baltimore	1900	2,488	83
Morgan State College*	Baltimore	1867	5,743	279
University of Maryland*	Eastern Shore	1970	771	60
MISSISSIPPI:				
Alcorn A & M College*	Lorman	1871	2,677	116
Jackson State*	Jackson	1877	5,058	300
Mississippi Industrial College	Holly Springs	1905	285	--
Mississippi Valley State College*	Itta Bena	1946	2,410	132
Rust College	Holly Springs	1866	747	42
Tougaloo College	Tougaloo	1869	750	65
MISSOURI:				
Lincoln University*	Jefferson City	1866	2,620	147
NORTH CAROLINA:				
Barber-Scotia College	Concord	1867	550	44
Bennett College	Greensboro	1874	582	71
Elizabeth City State University*	Elizabeth City	1891	1,084	82

States and Institutions*	Location	Year Founded	Enrollment	Faculty
NORTH CAROLINA (cont.):				
Fayetteville State University*	Fayetteville	1877	1,490	96
Johnson C. Smith University	Charlotte	1867	1,036	73
Livingstone College	Salisbury	1879	754	82
North Carolina A & T State University*	Greensboro	1891	4,445	274
North Carolina Central University*	Durham	1910	3,723	269
St. Augustine's College	Raleigh	1867	1,284	73
Shaw University	Raleigh	1865	1,061	84
Winston-Salem State University*	Salem	1892	1,623	109
OHIO:				
Central State University*	Wilberforce	1887	2,525	158
Wilberforce University	Wilberforce	1856	1,328	46
OKLAHOMA:				
Langston University*	Langston	1897	1,236	79
PENNSYLVANIA:				
Cheyney State College*	Cheyney	1837	2,362	210
Lincoln University*	Lincoln	1854	1,067	98
SOUTH CAROLINA:				
Allen University	Columbia	1870	456	66
Benedict College	Columbia	1870	1,487	88
Claflin College	Orangeburg	1869	795	55
Morris College	Sumter	1908	520	--
South Carolina State*	Orangeburg	1896	2,383	145
Voorhees College	Denmark	1897	736	46
TENNESSEE:				
Fisk University	Nashville	1865	1,413	120
Knoxville College	Knoxville	1875	1,039	100
Lane College	Jackson	1882	921	58
Le-Moyne College	Memphis	1870	712	56
Meharry Medical College	Nashville	1876	571	239
Morristown Normal & Ind. College	Morristown	1881	150	14
Tennessee State University*	Nashville	1912	4,576	276

States and Institutions*	Location	Year Founded	Enrollment	Faculty
TEXAS:				
Bishop College	Dallas	1881	1,561	142
Huston-Tillotson College	Austin	1876	717	58
Jarvis Christian College	Hawkins	1912	645	51
Paul Quinn College	Waco	1872	457	45
Prairie View A & M*	Prairie View	1876	4,115	--
St. Phillipps College*	San Antonio	1898	3,122	--
Texas College	Tyler	1894	511	39
Texas Southern University*	Houston	1947	6,174	260
Wiley College	Marshall	1873	510	41
VIRGINIA:				
Hampton Institute	Hampton	1868	2,587	208
Norfolk State College*	Norfolk	1935	5,678	300
St. Paul's College*	Lawrenceville	1888	512	43
Virginia College	Lynchburg	1888	91	--
Virginia State College*	Petersburg	1882	3,684	216
Virginia Union University	Richmond	1865	1,107	81
WEST VIRGINIA:				
Bluefield State College*	Bluefield	1895	1,117	83
West Virginia State College*	Institute	1891	3,590	154

MAJOR AFRO-AMERICAN ORGANIZATIONS

Alpha Kappa Alpha Sorority
5211 South Greenwood Avenue
Chicago, Ill. 60615
(312) 684-1282
Founded: 1908

Alpha Phi Alpha Fraternity
4432 Martin Luther King Drive
Chicago, Ill. 60653
(312) 373-1819
Founded: 1906

Black Academy of Arts and
Letters
475 Riverside Drive
New York, N.Y. 10027
(212) 663-4740
Founded: 1969

Congress of Racial Equality
(CORE)
200 West 135th Street
New York, N.Y. 10030
Founded: 1942

Congressional Black Caucus
House of Representatives
415 2nd Street N.E.
Washington, D.C. 20002
(202) 546-3425
Founded: 1971

Delta Sigma Theta Sorority
1707 New Hampshire Ave. N.W.
Washington, D.C. 20009
(202) 483-5460
Founded: 1913

Federation of Masons of the
World, Inc.
1017 East 11 Street
Austin, Texas 78702
(512) 477-5380
Founded: 1958

Frontiers International
1901 W. Girard Avenue
Philadelphia, Penn. 19130
(215) CE 5-5959

Girl Friends, Inc.
c/o Mrs. Jaqueline Robinson
4503 Crest Lane
McLean, Virginia 22101
Founded: 1927

Improved, Benevolent, Protective
Order of Elks of the World
1522 North 15 Street
Philadelphia, Penn. 19121
(215) GE 2-0150
Founded: 1929

Institute of the Black World
87 Chestnut Street S.W.
Atlanta, Georgia 30314
(404) 523-7805

Interracial Council for Business
Opportunity
470 Park Avenue
New York, N.Y. 10017
(212) 889-0880
Founded: 1963

Iota Phi Lambda Sorority
1940 McClure Avenue
Youngston, Ohio 44505
Founded: 1929

Kappa Alpha Psi Fraternity
2320 North Broad Street
Philadelphia, Penn. 19132
(215) 228-7184

Lamba Kappa Mu Sorority
    Marie G. Leatherman, Grand
        Basileus
    503 Trowbridge Street
    Detroit, Michigan 48202
    Founded: 1937

Leadership Conference on Civil
Rights
    2027 Massachusetts Ave. N.W.
    Washington, D.C. 20036
    (202) 667-3450
    Founded: 1949

National Alliance of Postal and
Federal Employees
    1644 11th Street N.W.
    Washington, D.C. 20001
    (202) 332-4313
    Founded: 1925

National Association for the
Advancement of Colored People
(NAACP)
    1790 Broadway
    New York, N.Y. 10019
    (212) 245-2100
    Founded: 1909

National Association of Black
Accountants
    P.O. Box 726 F.D.R. Station
    New York, N.Y. 10022
    Founded: 1970

National Association of Black
Social Workers, Inc.
    2008 Madison Avenue
    New York, N.Y. 10035
    (212) 348-0035
    Founded: 1968

National Association of College
Deans, Registrars & Admissions
Officers (Nacdrao)
    Albany State College
    Albany, Georgia
    (912) 555-1212
    Founded: 1923

National Association of Colored
Women's Clubs, Inc.
    1601 R Street N.W.
    Washington, D.C. 20009
    (202) DE 2-8160
    Founded: 1896

National Association for Health
Services Executives
    2600 Liberty Heights Avenue
    Baltimore, Maryland 21215
    (301) 523-4005
    Founded: 1968

National Association of Market
Developers
    201 Ashby St., N.W. Suite 306
    Atlanta, Georgia 30314
    Founded: 1953

National Association of Media
Women, Inc.
    157 West 126th Street
    New York, N.Y. 10027
    (212) 666-1320
    Founded: 1965

National Association of Negro
Business and Professional
Women's Clubs
    2861 Urban Avenue
    Columbus, Georgia 31907
    Founded: 1935

National Association of Real
Estate Brokers
  1025 Vermont Avenue N.W.
    Suite 1111
  Washington, D.C. 20005
  (202) 638-1280
  Founded: 1947

National Bankers Association
  1325 Massachusetts Ave. N.W.
  Washington, D.C. 20005
  (202) 628-8188
  Founded: 1927

National Baptist Convention, USA
  405 East 31st Street
  Chicago, Illinois 60616
  (312) 842-1081
  Founded: 1880

National Bar Association
  1314 North 5th Street
  Kansas City, Kansas 66101
  Founded: 1925

National Beauty Culturists
League, Inc.
  25 Logan Circle, N.W.
  Washington, D.C. 20005
  (202) 332-2695
  Founded: 1919

National Business League
  4324 Georgia Avenue N.W.
  Washington, D.C. 20010
  (202) 726-6200

National Committee of Black
Churchmen, Inc.
  110 East 125th Street
  New York, N.Y. 10035
  (212) 862-9628
  Founded: 1967

National Council of Negro
Women, Inc.
  1346 Connecticut Avenue N.W.
    Suite 832
  Washington, D.C. 20036
  (202) 223-2363
  Founded: 1935

National Dental Association
  P.O. Box 197
  Charlottesville, Virginia 22902
  (703) 293-8253
  Founded: 1913

National Funeral Directors and
Morticians Association
  802 Madison Avenue
  Baltimore, Maryland 21202

National Insurance Association
  2400 S. Michigan Avenue
  Chicago, Illinois 60616
  (312) 842-5125
  Founded: 1921

National Links, Incorporated
  118 Nelson Street
  Durham, North Carolina 27707
  (919) 682-4772
  Founded: 1946

The National Medical Association
  1717 Massachusetts Ave. N.W.
  Washington, D.C. 20036
  Founded: 1895

National Newspaper Publishers
Association
  3636 16th Street N.W.
  Washington, D.C. 20010
  (202) 332-7174
  Founded: 1940

National Pharmaceutical
Association
   Howard University College of
      Pharmacy
   Washington, D.C. 20001
   (202) 797-1341
   Founded: 1947

National Scholarship Service
and Fund for Negro Students
(NSSFNS)
   1776 Broadway
   New York, N.Y. 10019
   (212) 757-8100
   Founded: 1947

National Urban League
   55 East 52nd Street
   New York, N.Y. 10022
   (212) 751-0300
   Founded: 1910

N.A.A.C.P. Legal Defense and
Education Fund
   10 Columbus Cir. Suite 2030
   New York, N.Y. 10019
   (212) 586-8397
   Founded: 1939

Omega Psi Phi Fraternity
   2714 Georgia Avenue N.W.
   Washington, D.C. 20001
   (202) 667-7158
   Founded: 1911

Opportunities Industrialization
Center
   1225 North Broad Street
   Philadelphia, Penn.
   (215) 849-3010

Phi Beta Sigma Fraternity
   1006 Carroll Street
   Brooklyn, N.Y. 11225
   (212) 493-5425
   Founded: 1914

A. Philip Randolph Institute
   260 Park Avenue South
   New York, N.Y. 10010
   (212) 533-8000

Sigma Gamma Rho Sorority
   1254 25th Street
   Indianapolis, Indiana 46205
   Founded: 1922

Southern Christian Conference
   334 Auburn Avenue N.E.
   Atlanta, Georgia 30303
   (404) 522-1420
   Founded: 1957

Unitarian Universalist Caucus
   18 West Chelten Avenue
   Philadelphia, Penn. 19144
   (215) 438-7878
   Founded: 1967

United Mortgage Bankers of
America
   840 East 87th Street
   Chicago, Illinois 60519
   (312) 994-7200

MAJOR AFRO-AMERICAN PUBLICATIONS IN THE U. S.

City	Name	Established	Published
ALABAMA:			
Birmingham	Baptist Leader	1912	weekly
Birmingham	Mirror	1948	weekly
Birmingham	Times	1964	weekly
Birmingham	World	1932	weekly
Huntsville	The Weekly News	1969	bi-weekly
Mobile	Alabama Citizen	1954	weekly
Mobile	Beacon	1954	weekly
Selma	Mirror	1965	weekly
Selma	Sun-Post	1972	weekly
ARIZONA:			
Phoenix	Arizona Informant	1971	weekly
Phoenix	Arizona Tribune	1958	weekly
ARKANSAS:			
Little Rock	Southern Meditator Journal	1938	weekly
CALIFORNIA:			
Albany	Black Times	----	weekly
Altadena Pasadena	Eagle	1968	weekly
Bakersfield	Observer	1955	weekly
Berkeley	Post	----	weekly
Berkeley	Richmond Post	----	weekly
Berkeley	San Francisco Post	----	weekly
Berkeley	Seaside Post	----	weekly
Compton	Metropolitan Gazette	1946	weekly
East Palo Alto	Peninsula Bulletin	1966	weekly
Hayward	New Lady Magazine	----	monthly
Fresno	California Advocate	1967	weekly
Los Angeles	Central News-Wave Publications	1938	weekly
Los Angeles	Firestone Park News & Southeast News Press	1916	weekly
Los Angeles	Herald-Dispatch	1952	semi-weekly
Los Angeles	News	1959	weekly
Los Angeles	News Press	1962	weekly
Los Angeles	Sentinel	1934	weekly
Los Angeles	Soul Illustrated	----	bi-monthly

City	Name	Established	Published
CALIFORNIA (cont.):			
Los Angeles	United Pictorial Review	----	weekly
Los Angeles	Watts Star Review	1929	weekly
Menlo Park Ravenswood	Post	1953	weekly
Oakland	The Black Panther	1965	----
Oakland	California Voice	1919	weekly
Oakland	Post	1963	semi-weekly
Palo Alto	Black Times	1971	monthly
Pomona	Clarion	1970	weekly
Sacramento	Observer	1962	weekly
San Bernardino	Precinct Reporter	1965	weekly
San Diego	Voice and Viewpoint	1959	weekly
San Francisco	Metro	----	monthly
San Francisco	Sun Reporter	1944	weekly
Santa Ana	Orange County Star Review	1971	weekly
CONNECTICUT:			
Bridgeport	Harambee	1968	monthly
Hartford	Star	1969	weekly
New Haven	Star	1971	weekly
DELAWARE:			
Wilmington	Delaware Defender	1962	weekly
DISTRICT OF COLUMBIA:			
	Afro-American	1933	semi-weekly
	Capitol Spotlight	1953	weekly
	Informer	1964	weekly
	Journal of Negro Education	1932	quarterly
	Negro History Bulletin	1937	monthly
	New Observer	1960	weekly
	Tribune	1933	semi-weekly
FLORIDA:			
Ft. Myers	Star-News	1971	weekly
Ft. Lauderdale	Westside Gazette	1971	weekly
Ft. Pierce	Chronicle	1957	weekly
Jacksonville	Florida-Star-News	1951	weekly
Miami	Florida Courier	----	weekly

City	Name	Established	Published
FLORIDA (cont.):			
Miami	Times	1923	weekly
Orlando	Florida Sun	1932	weekly
Pensacola	Exposure	----	weekly
Pensacola	Times	1968	weekly
St. Petersburg	Weekly Challenger	1967	weekly
Sarasota	Weekly Bulletin	1959	weekly
Tampa	Florida Sentinel- Bulletin	1945	semi-weekly
Tampa	News Reporter	1958	weekly
West Palm Beach	Photo Illustrated News	1955	weekly
GEORGIA:			
Albany	Times	1964	weekly
Albany	Southwest Georgian	1940	weekly
Atlanta	Inquirer	1960	weekly
Atlanta	Atlanta Magazine	----	monthly
Atlanta	Voice	1966	weekly
Atlanta	Daily World	1928	4-days-week
Augusta	Voice	1970	weekly
Augusta	News Review	1971	weekly
Columbus	Times	1958	3-days-week
Savannah	Herald	1945	weekly
Thomasville- Tallahassee	News	1967	weekly
ILLINOIS:			
Chicago	Black Stars	----	monthly
Chicago	Bulletin	----	weekly
Chicago	Citizen	1965	weekly
Chicago	Courier	1959	weekly
Chicago	Daily Defender	1905	daily
Chicago	Defender	----	weekly
Chicago	Ebony	----	monthly
Chicago	Gazette	1950	weekly
Chicago	Independent Bulletin	1958	weekly
Chicago	Jet	----	weekly
Chicago	Metro News	1972	weekly
Chicago	Muhammad Speaks	1961	weekly
Chicago	Negro Traveler	----	monthly
Chicago	New Crusader	1940	weekly
Chicago	Woodlawn Booster	----	weekly
Chicago	Woodlawn Observer	----	weekly
East St. Louis	Crusader	1941	weekly

City	Name	Established	Published
ILLINOIS (cont.):			
East St. Louis	Monitor	1962	weekly
Evanston	North Shore Examiner	1968	bi-weekly
Maywood	Suburban Echo-Reporter	1964	weekly
Rockford	Crusader	1950	weekly
INDIANA:			
Gary	American	1927	weekly
Gary	New Crusader	1961	weekly
Gary	Info	1961	weekly
Indianapolis	Indiana Herald	1959	weekly
Indianapolis	Recorder	1895	weekly
South Bend	Reformer	1967	weekly
IOWA:			
Des Moines	New Iowa Bystander	1894	weekly
Waterloo	Defender	1963	bi-weekly
KANSAS:			
Wichita	Times	1970	weekly
KENTUCKY:			
Louisville	American Baptist	1880	weekly
Louisville	Defender	1933	weekly
LOUISIANA:			
Alexandria	News Leader	1962	weekly
Baton Rouge	News Leader	1952	weekly
LaFayette	News Leader	1970	weekly
Lake Charles	News Leader	1965	weekly
Monroe	News Leader	1962	weekly
New Orleans	Louisiana Weekly	1926	weekly
Shreveport	Sun	1920	weekly
MARYLAND:			
Baltimore	Afro-American	1892	semi-weekly
MASSACHUSETTS:			
Boston	Bay State Banner	1970	weekly
MICHIGAN:			
Detroit	Michigan Chronicle	1936	weekly

City	Name	Established	Published
MICHIGAN (cont.):			
Detroit	Pyramid	1942	quarterly
Detroit	Telegraph	1945	weekly
Jackson	Blazer	1962	weekly
Saginaw	Valley Star	1970	weekly
(Addendum)			
MINNESOTA:			
Minneapolis	Spokesman	1934	weekly
Minneapolis	Twin Cities Courier	1966	weekly
Minneapolis	Twin Cities Observer	1941	weekly
St. Paul	Recorder	1934	weekly
MISSISSIPPI:			
Greenville	Negro Leader	1962	monthly
Jackson	Advocate	1940	weekly
Jackson	Mississippi Enterprise	1939	weekly
Meridian	Memo Digest	1966	weekly
Natchez	News Leader	1971	weekly
New Albany	Community Citizen	1948	semi-monthly
MISSOURI:			
Kansas City	Black Progress Shopper News	1969	weekly
Kansas City	The Call	1919	weekly
Kansas City	Unique	----	monthly
St. Louis	American	1928	weekly
St. Louis	Argus	1912	weekly
St. Louis	Crusader	1963	monthly
St. Louis	Evening World	----	monthly
St. Louis	Metro Sentinel	1971	weekly
St. Louis	Sentinel	1968	weekly
NEBRASKA:			
Omaha	Everybody	----	monthly
Omaha	Star	1938	weekly
NEVADA:			
North Las Vegas	Voice	1968	weekly
NEW JERSEY:			
Camden	Jersey Beat	1955	weekly
Newark	Afro-American	1892	weekly
Newark	Nite Life	1958	weekly
Plainfield	Voice	1968	weekly

City	Name	Established	Published
NEW YORK:			
Brooklyn	N. Y. Daily Challenge	1972	semi-weekly
Brooklyn	N. Y. Recorder	1953	weekly
Buffalo	Challenger	1962	weekly
Buffalo	Criterion	1925	weekly
Hastings	Westchester County Press	1910	weekly
Jamaica	N. Y. Voice	1958	weekly
Mount Vernon	Westchester Observer	1947	weekly
New York	African Progress	----	monthly
New York	Amsterdam News	1909	weekly
New York	Contact	----	monthly
New York	Crisis	1910	monthly
New York	Journal of the National Medical Association	----	bi-monthly
New York	Manhattan Tribune	1968	weekly
New York	National Scene	----	monthly
New York	Our Colored Missions	----	monthly
New York	Say	1954	bi-weekly
New York	Voice of Missions	1892	monthly
Rochester	Communicade	1972	weekly
NORTH CAROLINA:			
Ashville	Southern News	1936	bi-weekly
Charlotte	Metropolitan News	1971	weekly
Charlotte	Post	1940	weekly
Charlotte	Quarterly Review of Higher Education Among Negroes	1933	quarterly
Charlotte	Star of Zion	1966	weekly
Durham	Carolina Times	1927	weekly
Gastonia	Gaston Times	1972	weekly
Greensboro	Carolina Peacemaker	1965	weekly
Raleigh	The Carolinian	1940	weekly
Wilmington	Journal	1945	weekly
OHIO:			
Bedford Heights, Cleveland	Metro	1955	monthly
Cincinnati	Call and Post	1950	weekly
Cincinnati	Herald	1956	weekly
Cleveland	Call and Post	1920	weekly
Columbus	Call and Post	1960	weekly
Toledo	Bronze Raven	1946	weekly
Youngstown	Buckeye Review	1937	weekly
Youngstown	Mahoning Valley Review	1967	weekly

City	Name	Established	Published
OKLAHOMA:			
Lawton	Community Guide	1971	weekly
Oklahoma City	Black Dispatch	1909	weekly
Tulsa	Oklahoma Eagle	1921	weekly
OREGON:			
Portland	Observer	1970	weekly
PENNSYLVANIA:			
Philadelphia	Afro-American Newspaper	1893	weekly
Philadelphia	Black Beauty	----	semi-annually
Philadelphia	Black Careers	----	bi-monthly
Philadelphia	National Beverage Leader	----	monthly
Philadelphia	Nite Life	1953	weekly
Philadelphia	Nite Owl	1957	weekly
Philadelphia	Nite Scene	1967	weekly
Philadelphia	Pride Magazine	----	bi-monthly
Philadelphia	Tribune	1885	semi-weekly
Pittsburgh	New Courier	1910	weekly
SOUTH CAROLINA:			
Charleston	Chronicle	1971	weekly
Orangeburg	Vue South	1964	monthly
TENNESSEE:			
Memphis	Tri State Defender	1951	weekly
Memphis	The Whole Truth	1935	monthly
Nashville	A.M.E. Christian Record	1846	weekly
Nashville	A.M.E. Church Review	----	quarterly
Nashville	The Broadcaster	1923	quarterly
TEXAS:			
Austin	Capital City Argus	1962	weekly
Austin	Inter-racial Review	1970	monthly
Dallas	Elite News	1960	weekly
Dallas	Key News	1966	weekly
Dallas	Weekly	1953	weekly
Fort Worth	Bronze Thrills	1951	monthly
Fort Worth	Como	1940	bi-weekly
Fort Worth	Hep	----	monthly

City	Name	Established	Published
TEXAS (cont.):			
Fort Worth	Jive	1951	monthly
Fort Worth	La Vida	1958	monthly
Fort Worth	Mind	1932	weekly
Fort Worth	Sepia	1954	monthly
Houston	Defender	1934	weekly
Houston	Forward Times	1960	weekly
Houston	Globe Advocate	1965	weekly
Houston	Informer	1892	weekly
Houston	Voice of Hope	1967	weekly
Lubbock	West Texas Times	1962	weekly
San Antonio	New Generation	1972	weekly
San Antonio	Register	1930	weekly
Tyler	Leader	1951	bi-weekly
Waco	Messenger	1927	weekly
VIRGINIA:			
Charlottesville	Albermarle Tribune	1954	weekly
Norfolk	Journal and Guide	1909	weekly
Richmond	Afro-American	1939	weekly
Richmond	Planet	1939	weekly
Roanoke	Tribune	1940	weekly
WASHINGTON:			
Seattle	Facts News	1961	weekly
Seattle	Medium	1970	weekly
Tacoma	Facts News	1969	weekly
WISCONSIN:			
Milwaukee	Courier	1963	weekly
Milwaukee	Star-Times	1971	weekly
Racine	Star News	1972	weekly

SIGNIFICANT SPORTS ACHIEVEMENTS BY AFRO-AMERICANS

Afro-American Batting Champions (National League)

	Year	Games	Hits	Average
Jackie Robinson, Brooklyn Dodgers	1949	156	203	.342
Willie Mays, New York Giants	1954	151	195	.345
Hank Aaron, Milwaukee Braves	1956	153	200	.328
Hank Aaron, Milwaukee Braves	1959	154	223	.355
Roberto Clemente, Pittsburgh Pirates	1961	146	201	.351
Tommy Davis, Los Angeles Dodgers	1962	163	230	.346
Tommy Davis, Los Angeles Dodgers	1963	146	181	.326
Roberto Clemente, Pittsburgh Pirates	1964	155	211	.339
Roberto Clemente, Pittsburg Pirates	1965	152	194	.329
Matty Alou, Pittsburgh Pirates	1966	141	183	.342
Roberto Clemente, Pittsburgh Pirates	1967	147	209	.357
Rico Carty, Atlanta Braves	1970	136	175	.366
Billy Williams, Chicago Cubs	1972	150	191	.333

Afro-American Batting Champions (American League)

	Year	Games	Hits	Average
Tony Oliva, Minnesota Twins	1964	161	217	.323
Tony Oliva, Minnesota Twins	1965	149	185	.321
Frank Robinson, Baltimore Orioles	1966	155	182	.316
Rod Carew, Minnesota Twins	1969	123	152	.332
Alex Johnson, California Angels	1970	156	202	.328
Tony Oliva, Minnesota Twins	1971	126	164	.337
Rod Carew, Minnesota Twins	1972	142	170	.318
Rod Carew, Minnesota Twins	1973	149	203	.350

Afro-American Scoring Leaders in the National Basketball Association

Player and Team	Points Scored	Avg.
Wilt Chamberlain, Philadelphia Warriors	2707	29.2
Wilt Chamberlain, Philadelphia Warriors	3033	37.9
Wilt Chamberlain, Philadelphia Warriors	4029	50.4
Wilt Chamberlain, San Francisco Warriors	3586	50.4
Wilt Chamberlain, San Francisco Warriors	2948	44.8
Wilt Chamberlain, Philadelphia 76ers	2534	34.7
Wilt Chamberlain, Philadelphia 76ers	2649	33.5
Dave Bing, Detroit	2142	27.1
Elvin Hayes, San Diego	2327	28.4

Afro-American Scoring Leaders in the National Basketball Association (cont)

Player and Team	Points Scored	Avg.
Lew Alcindor, Milwaukee Bucks	2596	31.7
Kareem Abdul Jabbar, Milwaukee Bucks	2822	34.8
Kareem Abdul Jabbar, Milwaukee Bucks		
Nate Archibald, Kansas City-Omaha		34.0

Afro-American Rebound Leaders in the National Basketball Association

Player and Team	Rebounds	Avg.
Maurice Stokes, Rochester	1256	
Bill Russell, Boston	1564	
Bill Russell, Boston	1612	
Wilt Chamberlain, Philadelphia	1941	
Wilt Chamberlain, Philadelphia	2149	
Wilt Chamberlain, Philadelphia	2052	
Wilt Chamberlain, San Francisco	1946	
Bill Russell, Boston	1930	
Bill Russell, Boston	1878	
Wilt Chamberlain, Philadelphia	1943	
Wilt Chamberlain, Philadelphia	1957	
Wilt Chamberlain, Philadelphia	1952	
Wilt Chamberlain, Los Angeles	1712	21.1
Wilt Chamberlain, Los Angeles		
Wilt Chamberlain, Los Angeles	1493	18.2
Wilt Chamberlain, Los Angeles	1572	19.2
Wilt Chamberlain, Los Angeles		18.6

Most Valuable Players

1969 West Unseld, Baltimore
1970 Willis Reed, New York
1971 Lew Alcindor, Milwaukee
1972 Kareem Abdul-Jabbar (Lew Alcindor), Milwaukee

Scoring Leaders

		Pts.	Avg.
1969	Elvin Hayes, San Diego	2327	28.4
1970	. . . .		
1971	Kareem Abdul-Jabbar (Lew Alcindor)		
	Milwaukee	2822	34.8
1972	Nate Archibald, Kansas City-Omaha		
	Kings	2719	34.0

Rebounding Leaders

	G	No.	Avg.
1969 Wilt Chamberlain, Los Angeles	81	1712	21.1
1970 Elvin Hayes, San Diego	82	1386	16.9
1971 Wilt Chamberlain, Los Angeles	82	1572	19.2
1972 Wilt Chamberlain, Los Angeles	82	1526	18.6

Assisting Leaders

	G	No.	Avg.
1969 Oscar Robertson, Cincinnati	79	772	9.8
1970 Lenny Wilkens, Seattle	75	683	9.1
1971			
1972 Nate Archibald, Kansas City-Omaha Kings	80	910	11.4

Afro-American Boxing Champions

Heavyweight

Name	Years Held
Jack Johnson	1908-1915
Joe Louis	1937-1949
Ezzard Charles	1949-1951
Jersey Joe Walcott	1951-1952
Floyd Patterson	1956-1959
	1960-1962
Sonny Liston	1962-1964
Cassius Clay (Muhammad Ali)	1964-1967*
Joe Frazier	1970-1973
George Foreman	1973-

Light Heavyweight

Battling Siki	1922-1923
John Henry Lewis	1935-1939
Archie Moore	1952-1961
Harold Johnson	1961-1963
Joe Torres	1965-1966
Dick Tiger	1966-1968
Bob Foster	1968-

*Title declared vacant by World Boxing Association when Ali refused induction into military.

Middleweight

Name	Years Held
Tiger Flowers	1926
Gorilla Jones	1931-1932
Sugar Ray Robinson	1951:
	1951-1952
	1955-1957: 1957: 1958-1960
Randy Turpin	1951
Dick Tiger	1962-1963: 1965-1966
Emile Griffith	1966-1968

Welterweight

Name	Years Held
Joe Walcott	1901-1904: 1904-1906
Young Jack Thompson	1931
Henry Armstrong	1938-1940
Sugar Ray Robinson	1946-1951
Johnny Bratton	1951
Kid Gavilan	1951-1954
Johnny Saxton	1954-1955: 1956
Virgil Akins	1958
Benny Kid Paret	1960-1961
Emile Griffith	1963-1966
Curtis Cokes	1966-1969

Lightweight

Name	Years Held
Joe Gans	1901-1908
Henry Armstrong	1938-1939
Beau Jack	1942-1944
	(New York)
Bob Montgomery	1944-1947
	(New York)
Ike Williams	1945-1947 (NBA)
	1947-1951
Jimmy Carter	1951-1952
	1952-1954: 1954-1955
Wallace Bud Smith	1955-1956
Joe Brown	1956-1962

Featherweight

Name	Years Held
George Dixon	1890-1899
Kid Chocolate	1932-1934
	(New York)
Henry Armstrong	1937-1938
Chalky Wright	1941-1942
Sandy Saddler	1948-1949: 1950-1957
Hogan Kid Bassey	1957-1959
Davey Moore	1950-1963

Bantamweight

Name	Years Held
George Dixon	1890-1892
Panama Al Brown	1929-1935
George Pace	1940
Harold Dade	1947
Jimmy Carruthers	1953-1954
(abandoned title)	

SPINGARN MEDALISTS

The Spingarn Medal awards were instituted by the late Joel E. Spingarn, chairman of the board of directors of the National Association for the Advancement of Colored People, in 1914. The awards are in the form of gold medals and are given each year to the Black American, who, according to the board, shall have reached the highest achievement in his field of activity.

The winners of the awards follow:

1915--Ernest E. Just, head of the department of biology, Howard University, for research in biology.

1916--Major Charles Young, U.S. Army, for organizing the Liberian constabulary and developing roads in Liberia.

1917--Harry T. Burleigh, composer and singer, for work in creative music.

1918--William Stanley Braithwaite, poet, literary critic, for distinction in literature.

1919--Archibald H. Grimke, president, American Negro Academy and former U.S. Consul at Santo Domingo, for achievement in politics and literature.

1920--William E. Burghardt DuBois, author, editor of The Crisis, for the founding of the Pan-African Congress.

1921--Charles S. Gilpin, actor, for his outstanding role in Eugene O'Neill's play, "Emperor Jones."

1922--Mary B. Talbert, former president of the National Association of Colored Women, for leadership in restoring the home of Frederick Douglass in Washington, D.C. as a shrine.

1923--George Washington Carver, head of the department of chemical research at Tuskegee Institute for his outstanding work in agricultural chemistry.

1924--Roland Hayes, tenor singer, for his international reputation in the music world.

1925--James Weldon Johnson, secretary of the NAACP, former U.S. Consul in Venezuela and Nicaragua, for achievement in literature.

1926--Carter G. Woodson, historian and educator, for collecting and publishing the records of the black in America.

1927--Anthony Overton, businessman, for his achievement in securing the admission of the Victory Life Insurance Company into New York State.

1928--Charles W. Chestnutt, novelist and short story writer, for his pioneer work in the field of literature, depicting the life of blacks in story form.

1929--Mordecai Wyatt Johnson, president of Howard University, for his success in administering the affairs of the University as its first black president.

1930--Henry A. Hunt, principal, Fort Valley High and Industrial School, Georgia, for his 25 years of work in the field of education in the South.

1931--Richard B. Harrison, actor, for his portrayal of the "Lawd" in Marc Connelly's play, "The Green Pastures."

1932--Robert Russa Moton, president of Tuskegee Institute, for his "thoughtful leadership in conservative opinion and action," his stand on education in Haiti, and his support of equal opportunity for the black in public schools.

1933--Max Yergan, a secretary of the YMCA, for his work among the natives of South Africa where he spent ten years, and his work in fostering inter-racial amity between white and black students.

1934--William Taylor Burwell Williams, field agent of the Jeanes and Slater Funds and dean of the college of Tuskegee Institute, for his work in education.

1935--Mary McLeod Bethune, president of Bethune-Cookman College, Florida, for her founding and building up of the school against great difficulties.

1936--John Hope, posthumously, president of Atlanta University, for his successes in the field of education.

1937--Walter White, secretary of the NAACP, for his outstanding work in leading the fight for the passage of a federal anti-lynching bill and for civil rights for black Americans.

1938--No award was given.

1939--Marian Anderson, contralto singer, for international fame in the field of music.

1940--Dr. Louis T. Wright, physician and surgeon, for outstanding work in surgery and civic affairs.

1941--Richard Wright, novelist, for writing one of the bestselling novels of the year, Native Son.

1942--A. Philip Randolph, president, Brotherhood of Sleeping Car Porters, for initiating the March-on-Washington demonstration.

1943--Judge William H. Hastie, for his distinguished career as a jurist and an uncompromising champion of equal justice, who resigned from his position as civilian aide to the Secretary of War in protest against discriminatory treatment of blacks in the armed forces.

1944--Dr. Charles R. Drew, professor of surgery, Howard University, for his work in blood plasma banks, which served as a model for the system of blood banks used throughout the country and in England.

1945--Paul Robeson, athlete, actor, singer, and scholar, for his achievement in theater and on the concert stage.

1946--Thurgood Marshall, attorney for the NAACP, for his contributions as a lawyer before the Supreme Court.

1947--Percy L. Julian, scientist, educator, and chemist, for his outstanding contribution to research in chemistry.

1948--Channing H. Tobias, minister, educator, civic leader, for his role in defending fundamental American liberties.

1949--Ralph J. Bunche, diplomat, for his distinguished scholarship in Myrdal study, The American Dilemma.

1950--Charles H. Houston, lawyer involved with fair employment practices, for his outstanding leadership in the legal profession.

1951--Mabel K. Staupers, nurse, for her contribution of the betterment of blacks in the field of nursing.

1952--Harry T. Moore, Florida coordinator for NAACP, posthumously, for his courageous fight for greater black political participation.

1953--Paul R. Williams, architect, for contribution to design and architecture.

1954--Dr. Theodore K. Lawless, dermatologist, for his outstanding work in research of skin and skin-related diseases.

1955--Carl Murphy, publisher, for his leadership role in employment, education, and recreation.

1956--Jack R. Robinson, athlete, for his leadership role in baseball.

1957--Martin Luther King, Jr., minister, civil rights leader, for his leadership in the Montgomery bus boycott.

1958--Mrs. Daisy Bates, civil rights leader, and publisher, and the Little Rock Nine, a group of students, for their struggle to effect school integration in Arkansas.

1959--Edward Kennedy (Duke) Ellington, musician, bandleader, composer, for his outstanding musical achievement.

1960--Langston Hughes, poet, lyricist, newspaper columnist, for his distinction as "black poet laureate."

1961--Kenneth B. Clark, educator, sociologist and psychologist, for his research in the field of psychology.

1962--Robert C. Weaver, economist, for his development of a doctrine of "open occupancy" in housing.

1963--Medger W. Evers, civil rights leader, posthumously, for his dedication to the "fight for freedom."

1964--Roy Wilkins, civil rights leader, for his contribution to "the advancement of the American people and the national purpose."

1965--Leontyne Price, lyric soprano, for her outstanding accomplishments in music.

1966--John H. Johnson, publisher, businessman, for his pre-eminence in black publishing.

1967--Edward W. Brooke, attorney, politician, for his distinguished career as a public servant and first black senator in the 20th century.

1968--Sammy Davis, Jr., entertainer, for his "superb and many-faceted talent."

1969--Clarence Mitchell, Jr., NAACP executive, for his meaningful contribution to the cause of civil rights.

1970--Jacob Lawrence, painter, for his eminence as an artist portraying black life and history on the American scene.

1971--Rev. Leon H. Sullivan, clergyman and organization head, for his inspirational guidance of his church to the social and economic needs of the black people.

1972--Gordon Parks, photographer, writer, filmmaker, and composer, for his multi-faceted creative achievements.

1973--Wilson C. Riles, superintendent of public instruction in the State of California for his outstanding contributions in the field of education.

1974--Alvin Ailey, innovative dancer and choreographer, for his creative and productive contributions to the dance.

1975--Hank Aaron, in recognition of his career in major league baseball.

1976--Judge Damon J. Keith, jurist, for his defense of constitutional principles as U.S. Federal District Court judge.

MUSEUMS AND MONUMENTS
OF
AFRO-AMERICAN INTEREST

NEGROES

Tuskegee Institute, George Washington Carver Museum (founded 1938), P.O. Box 40, Tuskegee, Ala. Mon.-Sat., 10-4; Sun., 1-4; closed holidays. Admission free.

George Washington Carver National Monument (founded 1952), P.O. Box 38, Diamond, Mo. Daily, 8:30-5; closed Christmas. Admission free.

Dunbar House, 219 Summit St., Dayton, Ohio. June-Sept. 15, weekends and holidays, 10-5; school groups by appointment, April-Sept. Admission: adults, 15 cents; children, 10 cents.

Chatham-Kent Museum (founded 1943; opened 1945), 59 William St. North, Chatham, Ontario, Canada. Tues., Thurs., Sat., 3-5, 7:30-9; first and third Sun., 3-5. Admission: adults, 25 cents; children, 10 cents; children accompanied by adults, free; group rates.

"Uncle Tom's Cabin" (founded 1948), Dresden, Ontario, Canada. April-Nov., daily, 10-sunset. Admission: adults, 50 cents; children, 10 cents; group rates.

Wilberforce University, Carnegie Library (founded 1953), Wilberforce, Ohio. Mon., Tues., Thurs., Fri., 9-4; Wed., 9-11, 1-4; Sat., 9-12; Sun., 5-7:30; Mon.-Fri. eves., 6-9. Admission free.

NEGRO ART AND MUSIC

Howard University Gallery of Art (founded 1930), College of Fine Arts, 2455 Sixth St., N.W., Box 1023 (1), Washington, D.C. Mon.-Fri., 9-5; Sat., 10-12; closed holidays. Admission free.

Museum of Negro History and Art, Chicago, Ill.

New Orleans Jazz Museum (founded 1961), 1017 Dumaine St., New Orleans, La. Tues.-Sat. and holidays, 10-5; Sun., 1-5; closed Christmas. Admission: 25 cents.

NEGRO HISTORY

American Society of African Culture, 15 East 40th St., New York City.

Association for the Study of Negro Life and History (founded 1915), 1538 Ninth St., N.W., Washington, D.C. 20001. Mon.-Fri., 8:30-5.

Soper Collection, Morgan State College, Baltimore, Md.

Stowe House, 2950 Gilbert Ave., Cincinnati, Ohio. June-Sept. 15, weekends and holidays, 9:30-5; school groups by appointment, April-Sept. Admission: adults, 15 cents; children 10 cents; school groups with teacher, free.

Harriet Beecher Stowe House, 73 Forest St., Hartford, Conn. Not open to the public.

The Old Slave Mart (founded 1938), 6 Chalmers St., Charleston, S.C. 29401. Mon.-Sat., 10-5 (winter); summer schedule varies; closed national holidays. Admission: museum, adults, 50 cents; children 6-12, 25 cents; art gallery, free.

SLAVERY

Stratford Historical Society (founded 1925), 967 Academy Hill, Stratford, Conn. Wed., Sat., Sun., 11-5 (May-Labor Day); Thurs., Fri., Sat., 1-5 (Labor Day-May 1); and by appointment. Admission: adults, 75 cents; children, 20 cents.

Wallace House (opened 1897), 38 Washington Place, Somerville, N.J. Tues.-Sat., 10-12. 1-5; Sun., holidays, 2-5; closed Thanksgiving, Christmas, New Year's. Admission: adults, 25 cents; children 5-12, 10 cents; school groups free.

Zebulon B. Vance Birthplace (founded 1959; open 1961), Reems Creek Road, Weaverville, N.C. Tues.-Fri., 9-5; Sat., Sun., 2-5 (April-Oct.); Wed., 9-5; Sun., 2-5 (Nov.-March); closed Thanksgiving, Christmas, New Year's. Admission: adults, 25 cents; children, 10 cents.

Sam Davis Memorial Association (founded 1927; opened 1930), Smyrna, Tenn. Mon.-Sat., 8-5; Sun., 1-5; closed Thanksgiving, Christmas. Admission: adults, 50 cents; children, 25 cents; group rates.

Colonel E. S. Robertson Home, U.S. Highway 81, Salado, Tex. Mar. 15-June 15, Sept. 15-Oct. 15, Mon.-Sat., 10-5; Sun., 1:30-5; closed holidays. Admission: adults, 75 cents; children, 60 cents.

University of Virginia, Orland E. White Research Arboretum (founded 1928), Boyce, Va. By appointment. Admission free.

Booker T. Washington National Monument (founded 1957; opened 1963), Virginia Route 122, 16 mi. N.E. of Rocky Mount, Va. Daily, 8-5; closed Christmas. Admission free.

Fort Malden National Historic Park (founded 1941), 312 Laird Ave., Amherstburg, Ontario, Canada. Mon.-Sat., 9-8; Sun., 12-8 (July, Aug.); Mon.-Sat., 9-5; Sun., 1-5 (May, June, Sept.); Mon.-Sat., 10-4:30; Sun., 1-4:40 (Oct.-Apr.); closed New Year's, Good Friday, Christmas. Admission free.

ABOLITION

Commodore Perry Memorial House and Dickson Tavern (opened 1963), 201 French St., Erie, Penna. Sat., Sun., 1-4; June 15-Sept. 15, daily 1-4. Admission: adults, 25 cents; children, 10 cents.

Rowland E. robinson Memorial Association (founded 1937; opened 1963), Ferrisburg, Vt. June-Sept., daily, 8-8.

Lincoln-Tallman Museum (founded 1951), 440 North Jackson St., Janesville, Wisc. May 15-Oct., Mon.-Sat., 9-5; Sun., 11-5. Admission: adults, 50 cents; 'children 12-18, 35 cents; under 12, 15 cents.

SELECTED QUOTATIONS

1688. *Quakers of Germantown, Pennsylvania, made the first formal protest against slavery in the Western Hemisphere.* February 11.

. . . There is a saying, that we should do to all men like as we will be done for ourselves. . . . Here [in America] is liberty of conscience, which is right and reasonable; here ought to be likewise liberty of the body. . . . But to bring men hither, or to rob and sell them against their will, we stand against. . . . Pray, what thing in the world can be done worse towards us, that if men should rob or steal us away, and sell us for slaves to strange countries; separating husbands from their wives and children. . . .

. . . have these poor Negroes not as much right to fight for their freedom, as you have to keep them slaves?

> George H. Moore, *Notes on the History of Slavery in Massachusetts* (New York, 1866), pp. 75-77.

1776. *Phillis Wheatley was invited by General Washington to visit him at his headquarters in Cambridge, Massachusetts, so that he might express appreciation for her poem in his honor.* February 28.

Miss. Phillis: Your favour of the 26th of October did not reach my hands 'till the middle of December. Time enough, you will say, to have given an answer ere this. Granted. . . .

I thank you most sincerely for your polite notice of me, in the elegant lines you enclosed; and however undeserving I may be of such encomium and panegyrick, the style and manner exhibit a striking proof of your great poetical Talents. In honour of which, and in a tribute justly due you, I would have published the Poem, had I not been apprehensive, that, while I only meant to give the World this new instance of your genius, I might have incurred the imputation of Vanity. This and nothing else, determined me not to give it place in the public prints.

If you should ever come to Cambridge, or near Head Quarters, I shall be happy to see a person so favoured by the Muses, and to whom Nature has been so liberal and beneficent in her dispensations. I am, with great Respect, etc.

> John C. Fitzpatrick, ed., *The Writings of George Washington from the Original Manuscript Sources 1754-1799*, Vol. 4 (Washington, 1938), p. 360.

1814. *General Andrew Jackson appealed to free Negroes to fight as part of the militia.* September 21.

PROCLAMATION

To the free colored inhabitants of Louisiana

Through a mistaken policy you have heretofore been deprived of a participation in the glorious struggle for national rights in which our country is engaged. This no longer shall exist.

As sons of freedom, you are now called upon to defend our most inestimable blessing. As Americans, you country looks with confidence to her adopted children, for a valorous support, as a faithful return for the advantages enjoyed under her mild and equitable government. As fathers, husbands, and brothers, you are summoned to rally round the standard of the Eagle, to defend all which is dear in existence.

Your country, although calling for your exertions, does not wish yo to engage in her cause, without amply remunerating you for the services rendered. Your intelligent minds are not to be led away by false representations.—Your love of honor would cause you to despise the man who should attempt to deceive you. In the sincerity of a soldier, and the language of truth I address you.

To every noble hearted, generous, freeman of color, volunteering to serve during the present contest with Great Britain, and no longer, there will be paid the same bounty in money and lands, now received by the white soldiers of the U. States, viz. one hundred and twenty-four dollars in money, and one hundred and sixty acres of land. The non-commissioned officers and privates will also be entitled to the same monthly pay and daily rations, and clothes furnished to any American soldier.

On enrolling yourselves in companies, the major-general commanding will select officers for your government, from your white fellow citizens. Your non-commissioned officers will be appointed from among yourselves.

Due regard will be paid to the feelings of freemen and soldiers. You will not, by being associated with white men in the same corps, be exposed to improper comparisons or unjust sarcasm. As a distinct, independent battalion or regiment, pursuing the path of glory, you will, undivided, receive the applause and gratitude of your countrymen.

To assure you of the sincerity of my intentions and my anxiety to engage your invaluable services to our country, I have communicated my wishes to the governor of Louisiana, who is fully informed as to the manner of enrollment, and will give you every necessary information on the subject of this address.

Headquarters, 7th military district,
Mobile, Sept. 21st 1814
Andrew Jackson,
Maj. gen, commanding
Niles' Weekly Register, Vol. 7, Dec. 3, 1814.

1817 *James Forten, Negro abolitionist, was chairman of the First Negro Convention held in Philadelphia.* January 23.
Esteemed friend. . . .

The African Institution met at the Rev. R. Allens the very night your letter came to hand. I red that part to them that wished them a happy New Year, for which they desired me to return you many thanks. I must now mention to you that the whole continent seems to be agitated concerning Colonising the People of Colour. . . . Indeed the People of Colour, here was very much fritened at first. They were afrade that all the free people would be Compelled to go, particularly in the southern States. We had a large meeting of Males at the Rev. R. Allens Church the other evening. Three thousand at least attended, and there was not one sole that was in favour of going to Africa. They think that the slave holders want to get rid of them so as to make their property more secure. However it appears to me that if the Father of all mercies, is in this interesting subject . . . the way will be made strate and clear. We however have agreed to remain silent, as the people here both the white & colour are decided against the measure. My opinion is that they will never become a people until they come out from amongst the white people, but as the majority is decidedly against me I am determined to remain silent, accept as to my opinion which I freely give when asked. . . .

I remain very affectionately
Yours unalterably,
James Forten
James Forten, *Letter of January 25, 1817,
in Paul Cuffe Papers*(New Bedford Library)

1829   *"Walker's Appeal," militant anti-slavery pamphlet published by David Walker, was distributed throughout the country and aroused the Negroes and provoked slave-holders.* January 18.

. . . Remember, Americans, that we must and shall be free and enlightened as you are, will you wait until we shall, under God, obtain our liberty, by the crushing arm of power? Will it not be dreadful for you? I speak Americans for your good. We must and shall be free I say, in spite of you. You may do your best to keep us in wretchedness and misery, to enrich you and your children, but God will deliver us from under you. And wo, wo, will be to you if we have to obtain our freedom by fighting. Throw away your fears and prejudices then, and enlighten us and treat us like men, and we will like you more than we do now hate you, and tell us no more about colonization {to Africa}, for America is as much our country, as it is yours.—Treat us like men, and there is no danger but we will all live in peace and happiness together. For we are not like you, hard hearted, unmerciful, and unforgiving. What a happy country this will be, if the whites will listen. . . . But Americans, I declare to you, while you keep us and our children in bondage, and treat us like brutes, to make us support you and your families, we cannot be your friends. You do not look for it, do you? Treat us then like men, and we will be your friends. . . .

David Walker, *Walker's Appeal, in Four Articles* (Boston, 1830), pp. 79-80.

1843   *Henry Highland Garnet made controversial speech at the National Convention of Colored Men in Buffalo calling for a slave revolt and a general strike.* August 22.

Brethren, it is as wrong for your lordly oppressors to keep you in slavery as it was for the man thief to steal our ancestors from the coast of Africa. You should therefore now use the same manner of resistance as would have been just in our ancestors when the bloody foot prints of the first remorseless soul-thief was placed upon the shores of our fatherland. . . .

Brethren, the time has come when you must act for yourselves. It is an old and true saving, "if hereditary bondsmen would be free, they must themselves strike the blow." You can plead your own cause, and do the work of emancipation better than any others. . . . Think of the undying glory that hangs around the ancient name of Africa—and forget not that you are native-born American citizens, and as such, you are justly entitled to all the rights that are granted to the freest. Think how many tears you have poured out upon the soil which you have cultivated with unrequited toil and enriched with your blood; and then go to your lordly enslavers and tell them plainly, that *you are determined to be free*. Appeal to their sense of justice, and tell them that they have no more right to oppress you than you have to enslave them. . . . Inform them that all you desire is FREEDOM and that nothing else will suffice. Do this, and forever after cease to toil for the heartless tyrants, who give you no other reward but stripes and abuse. If they then commence worth of death, they, and not you, will be responsible for the consequences. You had better far all die—*die immediately*, then live slaves, and entail your wretchedness upon your posterity. If you would be free in this generation, here is your only hope. However much you and all of us may desire it, there is not much hope of redemption without the shedding of blood. If you must bleed, let it all come at once—rather *die freemen than to live to be slaves*. . . .

Brethren, arise, arise! Strike for your lives and liberties. Now is the day and the hour. Let every slave throughout the land do this, and the days of slavery are numbered. You· cannot be more oppressed than you have bzen—you cannot suffer greater cruelties than you have already. *Rather die freemen than live to be slaves*. Remember that you are FOUR MILLIONS!

> *A Memorial Discourse by Rev. Henry Highland Garnet*, James M. Smith, ed. (Philadelphia, 1865), pp. 48-59

1862   *Charlotte Forten, Negro poet and teacher, arrived in St. Helena, South Carolina, to teach Negroes.* October 29.

. . . I never before saw children so eager to learn, although I have had several years' experience in New-England schools. Coming to school is a constant delight and recreation to them. They come here as other children go to play. The older ones, during the summer, work in the fields from early morning until eleven or twelve o'clock, and then come to school, after their hard toil in the hot sun, as bright and as anxious to learn as ever. . . .

> Charlotte Forten, "Life on the Sea Islands," *Atlantic Monthly,* XIII (March, 1864), p. 591.

1864   *In a duel between USS Kearsage and CSS Alabama off the coast of France, a Negro sailor, Joachim Pease, displayed "marked coolness," and won the Congressional Medal of Honor.* June 19.

{Joachim Pease, Seaman} served as seaman on board the U.S.S. *Kearsage* when she destroyed the *Alabama* off Cherbourg, France, 19 June 1864. Acting as loader during this bitter engagement, PEASE exhibited marked coolness and good conduct and was highly recommended by his divisional officer for gallantry under fire. General Order 45, Dec. 31, 1864.

> The United States Navy, *Medal of Honor, 1861-1949*, p. 43.

1868   *Fourteenth Amendment became part of the Constitution.* July 28.

No State shall make or enforce any law which shall abridge the privileges or immunities of citizens of the United States, nor shall any State deprive any person of life, liberty, or property without due process of law; nor deny to any person within its jurisdiction the equal protection of the laws.

> Amendment 14, Section 1 (1868).

1872   *P.B.S. Pinchback became Acting Governor of Louisiana on the impeachment of the Governor.* December 11.

. . . several Senators (I hope they are not Republicans) think me a very bad man. If this be true I fear my case is hopeless, for I am a bad man in the eyes of the democracy {and} weak-kneed Republicans. But of what does my badness consist? I am bad because I have dared on several important occasions to have an independent opinion. I am bad because I have dared at all times to advocate and insist on exact and equal justice to all Mankind. I am bad because having colored blood in my veins I have dared to aspire to the United States Senate, and I am bad because your representatives dared express the will of the people rather than obey the will of those who thought they were the peoples' Masters, when they elected me.

Friends I have been told that if I dared utter such Sentiments as these in public that I certainly would be Kept out of the Senate, all I have to say in answer to this, is that if I cannot enter the Senate except with bated breath and on bended knees, I prefer not to enter at all. . . .

> P.B.S. Pinchback, *Pinchback's Handwritten Manuscript: Notes for a Speech*, from Howard University's Moorland Collection (Washington, 1873).

1895 *Booker T. Washington delivered his famous "Atlanta Compromise"
address at Cotton Exposition in Atlanta, Georgia.* September 18.

. . . To those of my race who depend on bettering their condition in a foreign land or who underestimate the importance of cultivating friendly relations with the Southern white man, who is their next-door neighbor, I would say: "Cast down your bucket where you are"—cast it down in making friends in every manly way, of the people of all races by whom you are surrounded.

Cast it down in agriculture, mechanics, in commerce, in domestic service, and in the professions. . . . Our greatest danger is that in the great leap from slavery to freedom we may overlook the fact that the masses of us are to live by the productions of our hands, and fail to keep in mind that we shall prosper in proportion as we learn to dignify and glorify common labour and put brains and skill into the common occupations of life; shall prosper in proportion as we learn to draw the line between the superficial and the substantial, the ornamental gewgaws of life and the useful. No race can prosper till it learns that there is as much dignity in tilling a field as in writing a poem. It is at the bottom of life we must begin, and not at the top. Nor should we permit our grievances to overshadow our opportunities.

To those of the white race . . .were I permitted I would repeat what I say to my own race: "Cast down your bucket where you are." Cast it down among the eight millions of Negroes whose habits you know, whose fidelity and love you have tested in day when to have proved treacherous meant the ruin of your firesides. Cast down your bucket among these people who have, without strikes and labour wars, tilled your fields, cleared your forests, builded your railroads and cities, and brought forth treasures from the bowels of the earth. . . . Casting down your bucket among my people, helping and encouraging them as you are doing on these grounds, and to education of head, hand, and heart, you will find that they will buy your surplus land, make blossom the waste places in your fields, and run your factories. While doing this, you can be sure in the future, as in the past, that you and your families will be surrounded by the most patient, faithful, law-abiding, and unresentful people that the world has seen. As we have proved our loyalty to you in the past, in nursing your children, watching by the sick-bed of your mothers and fathers and often following them with tear-dimmed eyes to their graves so in the future, in our humble way, we shall stand by you with a devotion that no foreigner can approach, ready to lay down our lives, if need be, in defence of yours, interlacing our industrial, commercial, civil, and religious life with yours in a way that shall make the interests of both races one. In all things that are purely social we can be as separate as the fingers, yet one as the had in all things essential to mutual progress.

There is no defence or security for any of us except in the highest intelligence and development of all. If anywhere there are efforts tending to curtail the fullest growth of the Negro, let these efforts be turned to stimulating, encouraging, and making him the most useful and intelligent citizen. Effort or means so invested will pay a thousand per cent interest. These efforts will be twice blessed—"blessing him that gives and him that takes.". . .

Nearly sixteen millions of hands will aid you in pulling the load upward, or they will pull against you the load downward. We shall constitute one-third and more of the ignorance and crime of the South, or one-third its intelligence and progress; we shall contribute one-third to the business and industrial prosperity of the South, or we shall prove a veritable body of death, stagnating, depressing, retarding every effort to advance the body politic . . . .

The wisest among my race understand that the agitation of questions of social equality is the extremest folly, and that progress in the enjoyment of all the privileges that will come to us must be the result of severe and constant struggle rather than of artificial forcing. No race that has anything to contribute to the markets of the world is long in any degree ostracized. It is important and right that all privileges of the law be ours, but it is vastly more important that we be prepared for the exercises of these privileges. The opportunity to earn a dollar in a factory just now is worth infinitely more than the opportunity to spend a dollar in an opera house.

. . . I pledge that in your effort to work out the great and intricate problem which God has laid at the doors of the South, you shall have at all times the patient, sympathetic help of my race. . . .

                              Booker T. Washington, *Up From Slavery*
                              (New York, 1901), pp. 218-225.

1895   *Ida B. Wells compiled the first statistical pamphlet on lynching, The Red Record.*

. . . We demand a fair trial by law for those accused of crime, and punishment by law after honest conviction. No maudlin sympathy for criminals is solicited, but we do ask that the law shall punish all alike. We earnestly desire those that control the forces which make public sentiment to join with us in the demand. Surely the humanitarian spirit of this country which reaches out to denounce the treatment of Russian Jews, the Armenian Christians, the laboring poor of Europe. the Siberian exiles, and the native women of India—will not longer refuse to lift its voice on this subject. If it were known that the cannibals or the savage Indians had burned three human beings alive in the past two years, the whole of Christendom would be aroused, to devise ways and means to put a stop to it. Can you remain silent and inactive when such things are done in our own community and country? Is your duty to humanity in the United States less binding?

                              Ida B. Wells, *A Red Record* (Chicago,
                              1894), p. 97.

1896   *United States Supreme Court decision of* Plessy v. Ferguson *upheld doctrine of "separate but equal."* May 18.

This case turns upon the constitutionality of an act of the General Assembly of the State of Louisiana, passed in 1890, providing for separate carriages for the white and colored races. . . .

The first section of the statute enacts "that all railway companies carrying passengers in their coaches in this State, shall provide equal but separate accommodations for the white and colored races. . . .

The object of the [Fourteenth] Amendment was undoubtedly to enforce the absolute equality of the two races before the law, but in the nature of things it could not have been intended to abolish distinctions based upon color, or to enforce social, as distinguished from political equality, or a commingling of the two races upon terms unsatisfactory to either. Laws permitting, and even requiring, their separation in places where they are liable to be brought into contact do not necessarily imply the inferiority of either race to the other, and have been generally, if not universally, recognized as within the competency of the state legislatures in the exercise of their police power. The most common instance of this is connected with the establishment of separate schools for white and colored children, which has been held to be a valid exercise of the legislative power even by courts of States where the political rights of the colored race have been longest and most earnestly enforced. . . .

We consider the underlying fallacy of the plaintiff's argument to consist in the assumption that the enforced separation of the two races stamp the colored race with a badge of inferiority. If this be so, it is not by reason of anything found in the act, but solely because the colored race chooses to put that construction upon it. . . . The argument also assumes that social prejudices may be overcome by legislation, and that equal rights cannot be secured to the Negro except by an enforced commingling of the two races. We cannot accept this proposition. If the two races are to meet upon terms of social equality, it must be the result of natural affinities, a mutual appreciation of each other's merits and a voluntary consent of individuals. . . . Legislation is powerless to eradicate racial instincts or to abolish distinctions based upon physical differences, and the attempt to do so can only result in accentuating the difficulties of the present situation. If the civil and political rights of both races be equal, one cannot be inferior to the other civilly or politically. If one race be inferior to the other socially, the Constitution of the United States cannot put them upon the same plane.

163 U.S. 537 (1896).

1903   *W.E.B. DuBois published his* Souls of Black Folk.
    . . . in the history of nearly all other races and peoples the doctrine preached . . . has been that manly self-respect is worth more than land and houses, and that a people who voluntarily surrender such respect, or cease striving for it, are not worth civilizing.
    In answer to this, it has been claimed that the Negro can survive only through submission. Mr. Washington distinctly asks that black people give up, at least for the present, three things,—
    First, political power,
    Second, insistence on civil rights,
    Third, higher education of Negro youth,—
and concentrate all their energies on industrial education, the accumulation of wealth, and the conciliation of the South. . . . As a result of this tender of the palm-branch, what has been the return? In these years {since Booker T. Washington's Atlanta address} there have occurred:
    1. The disfranchisement of the Negro.
    2. The legal creation of a distinct status of civil inferiority.
    3. The steady withdrawal of aid from institutions for the higher training of the Negro.
    These movements are not, to be sure, direct results of Mr. Washington's teachings; but his propaganda has, without a shadow of a doubt, helped their speedier accomplishment. . . .
    {Negroes} do not expect that the free right to vote, to enjoy civic rights, and to be educated, will come in a moment, they do not expect to see the biases and prejudices of years disappear at the blast of a trumpet; but they are absolutely certain that the way for a people to gain their reasonable rights is not by voluntarily throwing them away and insisting that they do not want them; that the way for a people to gain respect is not by continually belittling and ridiculing themselves; that on the contrary, Negroes must insist continually, in season and out of season, that voting is necessary to proper manhood, that color discrimination is barbarism, and that black boys need education as well as white boys. . . .

W. E. Du Bois, *The Souls of Black Folk*
(Chicago, 1903), pp. 51-59.

1906   *Paul Laurence Dunbar, the poet, died in Dayton, Ohio.* February 9.

"We Wear The Mask"

We wear the mask that grins and lies,
It hides our cheeks and shades our eyes,—
This debt we pay to human guile;
With torn and bleeding hearts we smile,
And mouth with myriad subtleties.

Why should the world be over-wise,
In counting all our tears and sighs?
Nay, let them only see us, while
     We wear the mask.

We smile, but, O great Christ, our cries
To thee from tortured souls arise.
We sing, but oh the clay is vile
Beneath our feet, and long the mile;
But let the world dream otherwise,
     We wear the mask!

> Paul Laurence Dunbar, *Lyrics of Lowly Life* (New York, 1899), p. 167.

1956   *Manifesto denouncing U.S. Supreme Court ruling on segregation in public schools was issued by one hundred Southern Senators and Representatives.* March 11.

We regard the decision of the Supreme Court in the school cases as a clear abuse of judicial power. It climaxes a trend in the federal judiciary undertaking to legislate, in derogation of the authority of Congress, and to encroach upon the reserved rights of the states and the people.

The Original Constitution does not mention education. Neither does the Fourteenth Amendment or any other amendment. The debates preceding the submission of the Fourteenth Amendment clearly show that there was no intent that it should affect the systems of education maintained by the states. . . .

In the case of *Plessy v. Ferguson* in 1896 the Supreme Court expressly declared that under the Fourteenth Amendment no person was denied any of his rights if the states provided separate but equal public facilities. This decision has been followed in many other cases. . . .

This interpretation, restated time and again, became a part of the life of the people of many of the states and confirmed their habits, customs, tradition, and way of life. It is founded on elemental humanity and common sense, for parents should not be deprived by government of the right to direct the lives and education of their own children.

. . . the Supreme Court of the United States, with no legal basis for such action, undertook to exercise their naked judicial power and substituted their personal political and social ideas for the established law of the land.

This unwarranted exercise of power by the Court, . . . is destroying the amicable relations between the white and Negro races that have been created through 90 years of patient effort by the good people of both races. It has planted hatred and suspicion where heretofore there has been friendship and understanding.

Without regard to the consent of the governed, outside agitators are threatening immediate and revolutionary changes in our public school systems. If done, this is certain to destroy the system of public education in some of the states.

> *New York Times,* March 12, 1956, p. 19.

1963   *President Kennedy said nation faced "moral crisis" over Negro demands*
        for equality; pledged legislation to open public facilities for all (TV
        address). June 12.

. . . This Nation was founded by men of many nations and backgrounds. It
was founded on the principle that all men are created equal, and that the rights
of every man are diminished when the rights of one man are threatened.

Today we are committed to a worldwide struggle to promote and protect the
rights of all who wish to be free. And when Americans are sent to Vietnam or
West Berlin, we do not ask for whites only. It ought to be possible, therefore,
for American students of any color to attend any public institution they select
without having to be backed up by troops.

It ought to be possible for American consumers of any color to receive equal
service in places of public accommodation, such as hotels and restaurants and
theatres and retail stores, without being forced to resort to demonstrations in
the street, and it ought to be possible for American citizens of any color to
register and to vote in a free election without interference or fear of reprisal.

It ought to be possible, in short, for every American to enjoy the privileges
of being American without regard to his race or his color. In short, every American ought to have the right to be treated as he would wish to be treated, as
one would wish his children to be treated. But this is not the case.

The Negro baby born in America   today, regardless of the section of the
nation in which he is born, has about one-half as much chance of completing a
high school education as a white baby born in the same place on the same day,
one-third as much chance of completing college, one-third as much chance of
becoming a professional man, twice as much chance of becoming unemployed,
about one-seventh as much chance of earning $10,000 a year, a life expectancy
which is 7 years shorter, and the prospects of earning only half as much.

This is not a sectional issue. Difficulties over segregation and discrimination
exist in every city, in every State of the Union, producing in many cities a rising
tide of discontent that threatens the public safety. Nor is this a partisan issue.

In a time of domestic crisis men of good will and generosity should be
able to unite regardless of party or politics. This is not even a legal or legislative
issue alone. It is better to settle these matters in the courts than on the streets,
and new laws are needed at every level, but law alone cannot make men see
right.

We are confronted primarily with a moral issue. It is as old as the scriptures
and is as clear as the American Constitution.

The heart of the question is whether all Americans are to be afforded equal
rights and equal opportunities, whether we are going to treat our fellow Americans as we want to be treated. If an American, because his skin is dark, cannot
eat   lunch in a restaurant open to the public, if he cannot send his children to
the best public school available, if he cannot vote for the public officials who
represent him, if, in short, he cannot enjoy the full and free life which all of us
want, then who among us would be content to have the color of his skin changed
and stand in his place? Who among us would then be content with the counsels
of patience and delay?

One hundred years of delay have passed since President Lincoln freed the
slaves, yet their heirs, their grandsons, are not fully free. They are not yet freed
from the bonds of injustice. They are not yet freed from social and economic
oppression. And this Nation, for all its hopes and all its boasts, will not be
fully free until all its citizens are free.

We preach freedom around the world, and we mean it, and we cherish our
freedom here at home, but are we to say to the world, and much more im-
portantly, to each other that this is a land of the free except for the Negroes;

that we have no second-class citizens except Negroes; that we have no class or caste system, no ghettoes, no master race except with respect to Negroes?

Now the time has come for this Nation to fulfill its promise. The events in Birmingham and elsewhere have so increased the cries for equality that no city or State or legislative body can prudently choose to ignore them.

The fires of frustration and discord are burning in every city, North and South, where legal remedies are not at hand. Redress is sought in the streets, in demonstrations, parades, and protests which create tensions and threaten violence and threaten lives.

We face, therefore, a moral crisis as a country and as a people. It cannot be met by repressive police action. It cannot be left to increased demonstrations in the streets. It cannot be quieted by token moves or talk. It is a time to act in the Congress, in your State and local legislative body and, above all, in all of our daily lives.

It is not enough to pin the blame on others, to say this is a problem of one section of the country or another, or deplore it. A great change is at hand, and our task, our obligation, is to make that revolution, that change, peaceful and constructive for all.

Those who do nothing are inviting shame as well as violence. Those who act boldly are recognizing right as well as reality.

Next week I shall ask the Congress of the United States to act, to make a commitment it has not fully made in this century to the proposition that race has no place in American life or law. . . . .

John F. Kennedy, *Public Papers of the Presidents of the United States*, Vol. III (Washington, 1964), pp. 236-237.

SELECTED STATISTICAL ABSTRACT OF THE SOCIAL AND ECONOMIC STATUS OF THE AFRO-AMERICAN IN THE UNITED STATES

Adapted from, *Statistical Abstract of the United States 1970*

U.S. Department of Commerce
Bureau of the Census 1974
Current Population Reports

POPULATION: GROWTH, COMPOSITION, AND DISTRIBUTION

The black resident population increased by 1.4 million persons, or at an average annual rate of 1.6 percent, between April 1970 and April 1974. The average rate of growth during the 1960 decade was 1.8 percent per year. The lower annual rate of growth since 1970 reflects the declining birth rate among blacks. The most recent estimate of the black resident population was 24.4 million in April 1975.

During the last three decades (1940 to 1970) there were mass movements of blacks out of the South. However, since 1970 there appears to be a new emerging pattern of migration. There is some evidence that the South has been experiencing a decline in the volume of black outmigration and, at the same time, an increase in black inmigration. In fact, during the 4-year period 1970-74 the number of blacks 4 years old and over moving to the South closely approximated the number moving from the South—276,000 inmigrants versus 241,000 outmigrants.

After declining steadily for the last three decades, the proportion of blacks living in the South has leveled off at about 53 percent, reflecting the changing migration pattern.

From 1960 to 1970, overall population increases in central cities of metropolitan areas were a product of large gains in the black population, due both to inmigration and natural increase;[1] whereas the expansion of the suburbs (outside central cities) was overwhelmingly the result of the influx of the white population from the central cities.

Nevertheless, within the last 4 years the black population in the central cities experienced a slowdown in its rate of growth. Between 1970 and 1974, the black population in central cities increased at an annual rate of 1.6 percent, which was lower than that observed in the 1960's. The slowdown in the growth rate of the black population in cities can be attributed partly to the decline in the rate of natural increase, but also to an apparent decline in the rate of net inmigration. The white population registered a 1-percent annual decline in the central cities between 1970 and 1974.

As a result of modest increases in the black population and the exodus of whites, the proportion of blacks of the total central city population rose slightly over the 4-year period (22.3 percent in 1974 compared with 20.5 percent in 1970). Similar increases were noted for both the larger metropolitan areas (1,000,000 or more) and the smaller ones (under 1,000,000).

The suburban black population recorded some gains and increased at a higher annual rate (4.4 percent) than that for whites (1.8 percent). From the Current Population Survey, it is not possible to identify where the expansion of the black population occurred, i.e., whether it was primarily in predominantly black towns, such as Compton, California and East St. Louis, Illinois, located in the "suburbs," or distributed throughout the suburban areas, paralleling the suburban pattern of whites. In 1974, the number of blacks remained relatively small in suburban areas (outside central cities) and still comprised only 5 percent of the total suburban population.

Independent estimates of the total and black populations as of July 1973 are presented for the 15 States with the largest black population in 1970.

---

[1] Annexations also played an important role in the overall growth of cities in the 1960-70 period.

Table 1. Total Resident Population: 1900, 1940, 1950, 1960, 1965, and 1970 to 1974

Year	Millions of persons		Percent black
	Total	Black	
1900[1]......................	76.0	8.8	11.6
1940[1]......................	131.7	12.9	9.7
1950[1]......................	150.7	15.0	9.9
1960......................	179.3	18.9	10.5
1965......................	193.0	20.9	10.9
1970......................	203.2	22.6	11.1
1971......................	205.7	23.0	11.1
1972......................	207.8	23.4	11.3
1973......................	209.5	23.7	11.3
1974......................	211.0	24.0	11.4

Note: Data in this table are for the resident population as of April 1. Figures for 1965 and 1971-74 are estimates.

Data shown in this section are from several sources--decennial censuses, estimates of the resident population, and the Current Population Survey; therefore, figures in the tables may vary according to the source.

[1]Data exclude Alaska and Hawaii.

Source: U.S. Department of Commerce, Social and Economic Statistics Administration, Bureau of the Census.

Table 2. Change in the Population: 1960 to 1970 and 1970 to 1974

(Numbers in thousands)

Subject		Black	White
Total population:	1960......................	18,872	158,832
	1970......................	22,581	178,098
	1974......................	24,038	183,823
CHANGE, 1960 TO 1970[1]			
Number..		3,709	19,266
Percent..		19.7	12.1
Average annual rate..........................		1.77	1.13
Natural increase:			
Number..		3,841	16,557
Births..		5,948	32,543
Deaths..		2,107	15,986
Percent..		20.4	10.4
Average annual rate..........................		1.84	0.97
CHANGE, 1970 TO 1974[1]			
Number..		1,458	5,726
Percent..		6.5	3.2
Average annual rate..........................		1.56	0.79
Natural increase:			
Number..		1,263	4,276
Births..		2,169	11,094
Deaths..		905	6,817
Percent..		5.6	2.4
Average annual rate..........................		1.35	0.59

Note: Population figures are the resident population as of April 1. The base for the percent change is the population at beginning of period. Average annual change is per 100 mid-period population.

[1]Includes natural increase, net civilian immigration, and net movement of the Armed Forces to posts overseas.

Source: U.S. Department of Commerce, Social and Economic Statistics Administration, Bureau of the Census.

Table 3. Percent Distribution of the Population by Region: 1965, 1970, and 1974

Area and race	1965	1970	1974
BLACK			
United States.......millions..	20.9	22.6	23.5
Percent, total..................	100	100	100
South...............................	54	53	53
North...............................	38	39	39
Northeast.........................	18	19	18
North Central.....................	20	20	20
West................................	8	8	9
WHITE			
United States.......millions..	169.2	177.7	181.3
Percent, total..................	100	100	100
South...............................	27	28	29
North...............................	55	54	53
Northeast.........................	26	25	24
North Central.....................	29	29	28
West................................	17	18	18

Note: Data for 1965 and 1974 are based on the March Current Population Survey and exclude members of the Armed Forces in barracks and similar types of quarters. Data for 1974 also exclude inmates of institutions. The 1970 data are for the resident population as of April 1.

Source: U.S. Department of Commerce, Social and Economic Statistics Administration, Bureau of the Census.

Table 4. Interregional Migration of the Population 4 Years Old and Over:
March 1970 to March 1974

(Numbers in thousands. Minus sign (-) denotes decrease)

Migration status and race	South	Northeast	North Central	West
BLACK				
Inmigrants....................	276	88	96	172
Outmigrants..................	241	143	199	49
Net migration................	35	-55	-103	123
WHITE				
Inmigrants....................	3,055	930	1,692	1,913
Outmigrants..................	7,041	1,799	2,284	1,466
Net migration................	1,014	-869	-592	447

Source: U.S. Department of Commerce, Social and Economic Statistics Administration, Bureau of the Census.

BLACKS IN AMERICA

Table 5. Metropolitan and Nometropolitan Population: 1970 and 1974, and Change, 1960 to 1970 and 1970 to 1974

(Numbers in thousands. Minus sign (-) denotes decrease)

Subject	Metropolitan areas[1]			Non-metropolitan areas
	Total	Inside central cities	Outside central cities	
1970				
Black..........................	16,342	12,909	3,433	5,714
White..........................	118,938	48,909	70,029	56,338
1974				
Black..........................	17,878	13,777	4,101	5,748
White..........................	121,875	46,758	75,117	59,628
Change, 1960 to 1970				
Black:				
Number......................	4,031	3,273	758	-323
Percent.....................	31.6	33.2	26.4	-5.3
Average annual rate..........	2.7	2.9	2.3	-0.5
White:				
Number......................	14,762	64	14,698	4,156
Percent.....................	14.0	0.1	26.1	7.8
Average annual rate..........	1.3	(Z)	2.3	0.8
Change, 1970 to 1974				
Black:				
Number......................	1,536	868	668	34
Percent.....................	9.4	6.7	19.5	0.6
Average annual rate..........	2.2	1.6	4.4	0.1
White:				
Number......................	2,937	-2,151	5,088	3,290
Percent.....................	2.5	-4.4	7.3	5.8
Average annual rate..........	0.6	-1.1	1.8	1.4

Note: For comparability with data from the 1974 Current Population Survey, the 1970 census figures have been adjusted to exclude inmates of institutions and members of the Armed Forces living in barracks and similar types of quarters. Data for 1974 represent a five-quarter average centered on April 1974. Quarterly estimates for the months of October 1973, and January, April, July, and October 1974 were used. Central city data for 1974 exclude annexations since 1970.

Z Less than 0.05 percent.

[1]Standard metropolitan statistical areas are defined as of 1970, and exclude Middlesex and Somerset Counties in New Jersey.

Source: U.S. Department of Commerce, Social and Economic Statistics Administration, Bureau of the Census.

Table 6. Blacks as a Percent of Total Population, Inside and Outside Metropolitan Areas, by Size of Metropolitan Area: 1960, 1970, and 1974

(Data shown according to the definition and size of metropolitan area in 1970)

Type of residence	1960	1970	1974
United States..............................	10.6	11.1	11.3
Metropolitan areas[1].............................	10.7	11.9	12.5
Central cities................................	16.4	20.5	22.3
Central cities in metropolitan areas of--			
1,000,000 or more..........................	18.8	25.2	27.0
Less than 1,000,000.......................	13.2	14.9	16.9
Suburbs.......................................	4.8	4.6	5.0
Suburbs in metropolitan areas of--			
1,000,000 or more..........................	4.0	4.5	4.9
Less than 1,000,000.......................	5.9	4.8	5.1
Nonmetropolitan areas...........................	10.3	9.1	8.8
In counties designated metropolitan since 1970.	(X)	7.7	8.6

X Not applicable.
[1]Excludes Middlesex and Somerset Counties in New Jersey.

Source: U.S. Department of Commerce, Social and Economic Statistics Administration, Bureau of the Census.

INCOME

Summary of Recent Changes in Income and Poverty

The severe inflationary and recession pressures of 1974 adversely affected the economic situation for both the black and white populations. The average income level of black families in 1974 (after adjustment for increases in prices), declined over the 1973 average,[1] not statistically different from a similar decrease for white families.

Men were more severely affected by the inflation than women. In terms of real purchasing power, the median income of black men eroded during 1974; whereas that for black women barely kept pace with the increasing prices. The same relationship held true for white men and women.

In line with the sharp climb in unemployment rates for men in 1974, the proportion of black and white men with income who worked year round, full time decreased from 1973 to 1974. For both black and white women, the comparable proportions remained essentially unchanged between 1973 and 1974.

Reflecting the upsurge in unemployment, the number of whites in poverty rose by 1.1 million from 1973 to 1974—matching the large increase experienced during the economic slowdown of 1969-70. The Current Population Survey showed an apparent increase of 79,000 for blacks in poverty, however, the sampling variability was too large to determine if an increase actually occurred among the black population.

The number of black families below the low-income level remained constant between 1973 and 1974; white families in poverty increased during the year.

[1] The decline for black families was statistically significant at the 1.6 level of significance. See section on "Source and Reliability of the Data."

Income Levels and Selected Characteristics of Families and Persons

Inflation continued to erode the income levels of black and white families. In 1974, the median income of black families was estimated at $7,800, an increase of 7.4 percent over the 1973 level. However, after adjusting for the rise in prices, the 1974 median declined by approximately 3.2 percent over the 1973 median.[2] This was not statistically different from the 4.4 percent decline noted for white families. The median income of white families was $13,400 in 1974 (table 9).

The median income ratio of black to white families was 58 percent in 1974, showing no change from 1973.

The income status of blacks as reflected by the income distribution of blacks has hardly changed since 1970. Of the 5.5 million black families in March 1975, about 19 percent had high incomes in 1974 ($15,000 and above) and 38 percent had incomes of $10,000 and over. At the other end of the income scale, 23 percent of the black families had incomes under $4,000. In constant dollars, these proportions, as well as the median income level, have remained essentially unchanged from the corresponding 1970 figures (tables 11 and 12).

The overall income differential, as measured by the median income ratio, between black and white families has widened since 1970. In 1974, the average median income of black families was 58 percent of the median of white families; below the 1970 ratio of 0.61. However, the ratio has not changed since 1970, when such factors as family composition, labor force status of wife, etc. are taken into account. Some of the many factors which have an impact on the income ratio are discussed in the succeeding Income section "Income Ratio of Black to White Families." The index of income overlap, another measure of income comparability, was 0.72 in both 1974 and 1970, indicating no widening of the differentials between black and white income size distribution.

As was observed for the entire nation, the income disparity between black and white families, as measured by the median income ratio, has widened in the North and West since 1970—it was 67 percent in 1974 and 73 percent in 1970. On the other hand, Southern black families had maintained their income position relative to their white counterparts—the ratio was about 57 percent in both 1974 and 1970. Income levels in 1974 were still lower in the South than in the North and West (table 10).

In contrast to the decline in the overall median income ratio for families, the median income ratio of black to white persons has remained essentially unchanged since 1970. In 1974, the median income of black men ($5,400) was about 61 percent of the median income of white men—not statistically different from the 59 percent in 1970. For women, the ratio was about 90 percent in both 1974 and 1970.

Among men who worked year round, full time, the average income was 70 percent of the median income of the comparable group of white men, about the same as in 1970 (68 percent). However, black women who worked year round, full time made gains relative to their white counterparts—the income ratio in 1974 was 91 percent, up from the 82 percent in 1970 (table 13).

In addition to money income, some families receive nonmoney income from sources such as food stamps, surplus food, rent-free housing, expense accounts covering business transportation and facilities, payments for medical and educational expenses, etc. Information on one of these types of nonmoney income—food stamps—was obtained from a 1974 Current Population Survey.

Approximately 3.6 million households purchased food stamps in July 1974; of these, 1.4 million, or about 40 percent, were black households. In contrast to all households, households who received food stamps, regardless of the race of the head, were more likely to have a female head, to have lower incomes, and a greater proportion of large households (5 or more members) and to receive public assistance (table 14).

---

[2] Statistically significant at the 1.6 level of significance. See section on "Source and Reliability of the Data".

Table 7. Median Income of Families: 1950 to 1974

(In current dollars)

Year	Race of head			Ratio: Black and other races to white	Ratio: Black to white
	Black and other races	Black	White		
1950...................	$1,869	(NA)	$3,445	0.54	(NA)
1951...................	2,032	(NA)	3,859	0.53	(NA)
1952...................	2,338	(NA)	4,114	0.57	(NA)
1953...................	2,461	(NA)	4,392	0.56	(NA)
1954...................	2,410	(NA)	4,339	0.56	(NA)
1955...................	2,549	(NA)	4,605	0.55	(NA)
1956...................	2,628	(NA)	4,993	0.53	(NA)
1957...................	2,764	(NA)	5,166	0.54	(NA)
1958...................	2,711	(NA)	5,300	0.51	(NA)
1959...................	3,161	$3,047	5,893	0.54	0.52
1960...................	3,233	(NA)	5,835	0.55	(NA)
1961...................	3,191	(NA)	5,981	0.53	(NA)
1962...................	3,330	(NA)	6,237	0.53	(NA)
1963...................	3,465	(NA)	6,548	0.53	(NA)
1964...................	3,839	3,724	6,858	0.56	0.54
1965...................	3,994	3,886	7,251	0.55	0.54
1966...................	4,674	4,507	7,792	0.60	0.58
1967[1]................	5,094	4,875	8,234	0.62	0.59
1968...................	5,590	5,360	8,937	0.63	0.60
1969...................	6,191	5,999	9,794	0.63	0.61
1970...................	6,516	6,279	10,236	0.64	0.61
1971[2]................	6,714	6,440	10,672	0.63	0.60
1972[2]................	7,106	6,864	11,549	0.62	0.59
1973[2]................	7,596	7,269	12,595	0.60	0.58
1974[2]					
United States.........	8,265	7,808	13,356	0.62	0.58
South................	6,805	6,730	12,050	0.56	0.56
North and West.......	10,039	9,271	13,906	0.72	0.67
Northeast..........	9,399	8,788	14,164	0.66	0.62
North Central......	9,901	9,846	14,017	0.71	0.70
West..............	11,107	8,585	13,339	0.83	0.64

Note: Income figures for 1974 from the Current Population Survey conducted in March 1975, which recently became available, have been included in most of the tables in this section. A few of the tables in this section show income data for the year 1973. Data for 1959 are from the 1960 census; figures for the remaining years are from Current Population Surveys.

NA Not available. The ratio of black to white median family income first became available from this survey in 1964.

[1]Revised, based on processing correction.

[2]Based on 1970 census population controls; therefore, not strictly comparable to data for earlier years.

Source: U.S. Department of Commerce, Social and Economic Statistics Administration Bureau of the Census.

Income Ratio of Black to White Families

As noted previously, the median income ratio of black to white families has declined in the 1970's, after a rise in the mid and late 1960's. The decline in the black-white median income ratio reflects many interrelated factors according to a recent Current Population Report on consumer income issued by the Bureau.[3] The subsequent discussion presents some of the findings of that study; further information may be obtained by consulting the specific report.

Differential changes in the proportion of black and white multiple earner families and work experience patterns of family members appear to be among the more important factors contributing to the decrease in the black-white median income ratio since 1970. In turn, the variations in these two factors are partially the result of changes in (1) family composition, such as the proportion of husband-wife families with wives in the paid labor force and (2) the proportion of families headed by women.

The analysis which follows does not propose to explain all the reasons for these changes or all the underlying causes for the decline in the median income ratio. There are, undoubtedly, social and economic forces, such as changing attitudes, inflationary pressures, economic slowdown in 1969-1970, and the economic recession in 1974, which have had divers impacts upon the black and white communities.

Families With Wives in the Paid Labor Force.

Between 1970 and 1974, the proportion of black families with wives in the paid labor force declined from 36 to 33 percent; whereas, the proportion for their white counterparts increased from 34 to 37 percent. Changes in the proportion of all families with working wives are a result of changes in first, the proportion of all families which are husband-wife families and, second, the proportion of husband-wife families who have working wives (table 15).

As is noted in the Family section of this report, black husband-wife families as a percent of all black families have declined; virtually no changes have been observed for their white counterparts during the period 1970 to 1974 (income year).   The husband-wife families generally have median incomes which are higher than those of other types of families, primarily because they are more likely to have at least two earners. In 1974, black husband-wife families had a median income of $12,982 compared to $7,942 for black families headed by a male with no wife present and $4,465 for black families headed by a female. Thus, the decline in the proportion of black husband-wife families would have a downward influence upon the median income of all black families (table 16).

In the past, not only have proportionally more black than white wives worked to supplement the income resources of their families, but their contributions have been greater. Since 1970, the proportion of black husband-wife families with wives in the paid labor force has fluctuated; however, the percentage in 1974 (54 percent) was the same as that in 1970. During the same time period, the proportion for their white counterparts had increased from 38 to 42 percent. (From 1967 to 1970, both racial groups had experienced increases in this proportion.) The income levels of black husband-wife families with a wife in the paid labor force had risen from 1970 to 1974; but, these families have not improved their income status relative to comparable white families. (Black to white income ratio was about 78 percent for these families in both 1970 and 1974.) Between 1970 and 1974, the decline in the proportion of black husband-wife families has reduced the proportion of all black families with wives in the paid labor force. This pattern combined with changes which have occurred among white families has produced a downward effect upon the overall income ratio of black to white families in the '70's.

Families Headed by Women and Men.

Among families headed by women, the income ratio of black to white did not show a statistically significant change from 1970 to 1974 (62 percent in 1970 and 61 percent in 1974). The same pattern occurred among families headed by men; yet the overall income ratio of black to white families declined. This contradiction can be explained by differential changes in the proportion of black and white families headed

---

[3] See **Current Population Reports,** Series P-60, No. 97, "Money Income in 1973 of Families and Persons in the United States," pp. 5-12.

Families Headed by Women and Men—Continued

by women and men and incomes received by these families. The greater increase (1970 to 1974) in female heads among black families compared with white families is documented in the Family section of this report. Families headed by women generally receive less income than those headed by men.

Work Experience of the Family Head.[4]

Shifts have been observed in the work experience patterns between black and white families. The proportion of black families with a head who worked the previous year declined from 78 percent in 1970 to 73 percent in 1974, whereas that for white families dropped slightly from 84 to 82 percent. The reduction for blacks was the result of declines in the proportion who worked among both male and female heads of families. For whites the proportion of female heads who worked in the preceeding year did not change from 1970 to 1974; in contrast, a decline was noted for male heads.

As generally assumed, families with heads who held a job the previous year had higher incomes than families whose head did not have a job. Consequently, the relatively larger decline from 1970 to 1974 in the proportion of black heads who had gainful employment the previous year, than the decline for their white counterparts, had a negative effect upon the black-white income ratio.

Number of Earners Per Family.

Historically, black families have had a greater proportion of multiple earners than white families. However, from 1970 to 1974, the proportion of black families with 2 or more earners decreased from 55 percent in 1970 to 48 percent in 1974, falling below the 54 percent observed for white families in 1974.

The decline in multiple-earner families reflects both the changes in the composition of black families and the work patterns of black wives. Traditionally, most two-earner families were husband-wife families in which both husband and wife were earners.

In the past, multiple-earner families have been primarily responsible for the upgrading of income levels among black families. The decline (1970-74) in this proportion had a strong negative effect on the overall income level of black families.

[4]See **Current Population Reports,** Series P-60, No. 97, "Money Income in 1973 of Families and Persons in the United States," and forthcoming 1974 consumer income report.

Table 8. Median Family Income in 1959, 1969, 1970, and 1973 for All Black Families and Black Husband-Wife Families as a Percent of Corresponding White Families by Age of Head and Region

Area and year	All families		Husband-wife families	
	Total	Head under 35 years	Total	Head under 35 years
UNITED STATES				
1959	51	54	57	62
1969	61	66	72	80
1970	61	65	73	82
1973	58	62	74	88
NORTH AND WEST				
1959	71	68	76	78
1969	73	74	86	91
1970	74	70	88	96
1973	65	61	86	93
SOUTH				
1959	46	50	50	55
1969	57	62	65	73
1970	57	62	66	74
1973	56	66	67	87

Source: U.S. Department of Commerce, Social and Economic Statistics Administration, Bureau of the Census.

Low Income

There were 7.5 million blacks and 16.3 million whites below the poverty or low-income level in 1974. The apparent increase of 79,000 over the 1973 number of low-income blacks was not statistically significant. Sampling variability was too large to measure whether a change in the number of low-income blacks actually occurred. An increase of 1.1 million occurred for low-income white persons. The 1974 figures cover the period when the economy began its sharp downturn.

Since 1970, the number of low-income blacks, according to the CPS, has moved within a narrow range; during the 1960's a downward trend prevailed.

In 1974, low-income blacks comprised 31 percent of the black population, more than three times the comparable proportion of 9 percent for the white population.

The number of poor black families in 1974 was about the same as the 1973 figure; the number of low-income white families increased, returning to the 1972 level. After a rise at the very beginning of the decade (1969-70), the number of poor black families began to level off in the 1970's and has remained the same for the last 3 years. The trend represents a mixed composite of declines among low-income black families headed by men and increases among those headed by women.

Female heads have comprised an increasing proportion of both black and white low-income families, however, female heads have become an overwhelming majority only among low-income black families. At the beginning of the decade, about 56 percent of all poor black families were headed by women; by 1974, the proportion had grown to 67 percent. This proportion rose as a result of both the decline in the number of low-income black families headed by men and the concomitant increase in the numbers headed by women

Female heads of low-income families were less likely than the male heads to have worked. In 1973, about 38 percent of poor black female heads of families held a job sometime during the year and about 10 percent worked year round, full time. For black male heads of low-income families, the corresponding figures were 65 percent and 27 percent, respectively. Of the female heads not working, 7 out of 10 reported keeping house as their main reason for not working. The presence of children and often the lack of adequate low-cost day care facilities are factors which affect the ability of low-income female heads to seek gainful employment. As most of the poor male heads have wives present, these factors are not delimiting to them.

Among blacks, the low-income families were more likely than those above the poverty level to have one or no earners in the family. For example, about 42 percent of poor black families had one earner in 1973; the comparable proportion for black families above the low-income level was 33 percent. Also, the proportion of low-income black families with no earners (38 percent) was more than five times that for those above the poverty line. Moreover, among poor black families with multi-earners, there is some evidence that the second earner is usually not the wife, but another relative of the head; whereas among those above the low-income level, the wife is usually the secondary earner.

Since a sizable proportion of both black and white poor families had no earners, a substantial number had received unearned income in 1973. For black families below the low-income level without earnings, public assistance was the major source of unearned income; whereas, among white families, public assistance and Social Security were the two major sources of unearned income.

Table 9. Persons Below the Low-Income Level: 1959 to 1974

(Persons as of the following year)

Year	Number (thousands)			Percent below the low-income level		
	Black and other races	Black	White	Black and other races	Black	White
1959......................	10,430	9,927	28,336	53.3	55.1	18.1
1960......................	11,542	(NA)	28,309	55.9	(NA)	17.8
1961......................	11,738	(NA)	27,890	56.1	(NA)	17.4
1962......................	11,953	(NA)	26,672	55.8	(NA)	16.4
1963......................	11,198	(NA)	25,238	51.0	(NA)	15.3
1964......................	11,098	(NA)	24,957	49.6	(NA)	14.9
1965......................	10,689	(NA)	22,496	47.1	(NA)	13.3
1966[1]......................	9,220	8,867	19,290	39.8	41.8	11.3
1967......................	8,786	8,486	18,983	37.2	39.3	11.0
1968......................	7,994	7,616	17,395	33.5	34.7	10.0
1969[2]......................	7,488	7,095	16,659	31.0	32.2	9.5
1970[2]......................	7,936	7,548	17,484	32.0	33.5	9.9
1971[2]......................	7,780	7,396	17,780	30.9	32.5	9.9
1972[2]......................	8,257	7,710	16,203	31.9	33.3	9.0
1973[2]......................	7,831	7,388	15,142	29.6	31.4	8.4
1974[2]......................	7,970	7,467	16,290	29.5	31.4	8.9

LABOR FORCE

Recent Labor Force Developments

The employment situation for both black and white workers deteriorated during 1974 and early 1975 in line with the general downturn in the economy. Large increases in unemployment coupled with fairly widespread cutbacks in employment were experienced by both races. In contrast, there had been substantial improvements in employment for blacks and whites between 1972 and 1973.

Unemployment rates for both blacks and whites had declined to 3-½ year lows in the third and fourth quarters of 1973 and were 8.6 percent and 4.3 percent (seasonally adjusted), respectively, during the fourth quarter of 1973. As labor market conditions deteriorated, jobless rates surged during late 1974 and early 1975, reaching 13.7 percent for black and other races and 7.6 percent for whites in the first quarter of 1975. For adult men the jobless rate for both black and other races and whites doubled from late 1973, and was 11.1 percent and 5.8 percent, respectively, during the first quarter of 1975. For teenagers, the jobless rate for black and other races reached 39.8 percent in early 1975, compared with 18.0 percent for whites (tables 30 and 31).

The steep rise in unemployment was accompanied by sharp cutbacks in employment for workers of both races. Employment, which stood at 9 million for black and other races and 75.2 million for whites during the first quarter of 1975, was down sharply from high levels posted in early and mid-1974.

Paralleling these developments in employment and unemployment were increases in the number of persons of both white and black and other races who were nonparticipants in the labor force. Of particular interest within this group are those persons not in the labor force due to discouragement over job prospects.[1] (These persons, often called the "hidden unemployed," want jobs but are not looking for work because they believe their search would be in vain.) Their number, which had averaged about 525,000 white and 160,000 persons of black and other races in 1974, began to rise sharply in late 1974 and reached levels of about 800,000 and 315,000, respectively, during the first quarter of 1975. Among persons not in the labor force in early 1975, 4.4 percent of the black and other races and 1.6 percent of whites were discouraged workers.

Note: Consistent with the overall plan of this report, the section on Labor Force and Business Ownership focuses primarily on the situation in 1974 and past trends in the status of black workers. Because of significant economic developments in 1974 and early 1975, with resulting changes in the employment situation, limited quarterly data for 1973, 1974, and 1975 have been included in this section. These data provide the basis for a more current assessment of the employment status of blacks relative to whites.

[1] Shown as "think cannot get job" on table 32.

Table 10. EMPLOYMENT STATUS OF THE NONINSTITUTIONAL POPULATION, BY SEX AND RACE: 1950 to 1974

[In thousands of persons 16 years old and over. Annual figures are averages of monthly figures. See *Historical Statistics, Colonial Times to 1957*, series D 1–14 and D 20, for similar but not exactly comparable data]

YEAR OR MONTH, SEX, AND RACE	Total noninstitutional population	LABOR FORCE								Not in labor force [1]
		Total, including Armed Forces	Percent of population	Civilian labor force						
				Total	Employed			Unemployed		
					Total	Agricultural	Nonagricultural	Number	Percent	
TOTAL										
1950	106,645	63,858	59.9	62,208	58,920	7,160	51,760	3,288	5.3	42,787
1955	112,732	68,072	60.4	65,023	62,171	6,449	55,724	2,852	4.4	44,660
1960	119,759	72,142	60.2	69,628	65,778	5,458	60,318	3,852	5.5	47,617
1965	129,236	77,178	59.7	74,455	71,088	4,361	66,726	3,366	4.5	52,058
1968	135,562	82,272	60.7	78,737	75,920	3,817	72,103	2,817	3.6	53,291
1969	137,841	84,240	61.1	80,734	77,902	3,606	74,296	2,832	3.5	53,602
1970	140,182	85,903	61.3	82,715	78,627	3,462	75,165	4,088	4.9	54,280
1971	142,596	86,929	61.0	84,113	79,120	3,387	75,732	4,993	5.9	55,666
1972	145,775	88,991	61.0	86,542	81,702	3,472	78,230	4,840	5.6	56,785
1973	148,263	91,040	61.4	88,714	84,409	3,452	80,957	4,304	4.9	57,222
1974, Apr	150,283	91,736	61.0	89,493	85,192	3,437	81,756	4,301	4.8	58,547
MALE										
1950	52,352	45,446	86.8	43,819	41,580	6,001	35,578	2,239	5.1	6,906
1955	55,122	47,488	86.2	44,475	42,621	5,265	37,357	1,854	4.2	7,634
1960	58,144	48,870	84.0	46,388	43,904	4,472	39,431	2,486	5.4	9,274
1965	62,473	50,946	81.5	48,255	46,340	3,547	42,792	1,914	4.0	11,527
1968	65,345	53,030	81.2	49,533	48,114	3,157	44,957	1,419	2.9	12,315
1969	66,365	53,688	80.9	50,221	48,818	2,963	45,855	1,403	2.8	12,677
1970	67,409	54,343	80.6	51,195	48,960	2,861	46,099	2,235	4.4	13,066
1971	68,512	54,797	80.0	52,021	49,245	2,790	46,455	2,776	5.3	13,715
1972	69,864	55,671	79.7	53,265	50,630	2,839	47,791	2,635	4.9	14,193
1973	71,020	56,479	79.5	54,203	51,963	2,833	49,130	2,240	4.1	14,541
1974, Apr	71,993	56,507	78.5	54,327	51,927	2,887	49,040	2,401	4.4	15,486
Negro and other:[2]										
1955	[3]5,034	(NA)	[3]85.0	4,279	3,903	668	3,235	376	8.8	755
1960	[3]5,595	(NA)	[3]83.0	4,645	4,148	620	3,529	497	10.7	951
1965	6,330	5,084	80.3	4,855	4,496	463	4,033	359	7.4	1,246
1968	6,755	5,322	78.8	4,979	4,702	353	4,350	277	5.6	1,434
1969	6,918	5,404	78.1	5,036	4,770	309	4,461	266	5.3	1,513
1970	7,098	5,507	77.6	5,182	4,803	303	4,500	379	7.3	1,591
1971	7,266	5,533	75.9	5,220	4,746	271	4,475	474	9.1	1,753
1972	7,533	5,630	74.7	5,335	4,861	264	4,596	475	8.9	1,902
1973	7,845	5,868	74.8	5,555	5,133	255	4,878	423	7.6	1,977
1974, Apr	8,058	5,903	73.3	5,578	5,125	238	4,887	454	8.1	2,154
FEMALE										
1950	54,293	18,412	33.9	18,389	17,340	1,159	16,182	1,049	5.7	35,881
1955	57,610	20,584	35.7	20,548	19,550	1,184	18,367	998	4.9	37,026
1960	61,615	23,272	37.8	23,240	21,874	986	20,887	1,366	5.9	38,343
1965	66,763	26,232	39.3	26,200	24,748	814	23,934	1,452	5.5	40,531
1968	70,217	29,242	41.6	29,204	27,807	660	27,147	1,397	4.8	40,976
1969	71,476	30,551	42.7	30,513	29,084	643	28,441	1,429	4.7	40,924
1970	72,774	31,560	43.4	31,520	29,667	601	29,066	1,853	5.9	41,214
1971	74,084	32,132	43.4	32,091	29,875	598	29,277	2,217	6.9	41,952
1972	75,911	33,320	43.9	33,277	31,072	633	30,439	2,205	6.6	42,591
1973	77,242	34,561	44.7	34,510	32,446	619	31,827	2,064	6.0	42,681
1974, Apr	78,290	35,229	45.0	35,165	33,265	549	32,716	1,900	5.4	43,062
Negro and other:[2]										
1955	[3]5,772	(NA)	[3]46.1	2,663	2,438	288	2,150	225	8.4	3,109
1960	[3]6,369	(NA)	[3]48.2	3,069	2,779	248	2,530	290	9.4	3,300
1965	7,133	3,467	48.6	3,464	3,147	165	2,982	317	9.2	3,666
1968	7,670	3,784	49.3	3,780	3,467	90	3,377	313	8.3	3,886
1969	7,877	3,922	49.8	3,918	3,614	78	3,536	304	7.8	3,955
1970	8,114	4,019	49.5	4,015	3,642	65	3,577	373	9.3	4,095
1971	8,351	4,107	49.2	4,102	3,658	56	3,601	445	10.8	4,243
1972	8,736	4,254	48.7	4,249	3,767	47	3,721	482	11.3	4,481
1973	9,100	4,476	49.1	4,470	3,999	53	3,945	471	10.5	4,632
1974, Apr	9,394	4,508	48.0	4,499	4,117	29	4,088	382	8.5	4,886

NA Not available.   [1] Includes "other", not shown separately.   [2] Excludes white.
[3] Civilian noninstitutional population.

Source: U.S. Bureau of Labor Statistics, *Employment and Earnings*, monthly.

Black-Owned Businesses

Advances were made in black entrepreneurship during the 3-year period 1969-72. By 1972 there were 195,000 black-owned business enterprises with total receipts of $7.2 million, representing nearly a 20-percent increase in number of firms and approximately a 60-percent increase in gross receipts since 1969. The considerable increase in gross receipts reflects both the general inflation in prices and some real increase in volume of sales and services.

As in 1969, nearly all black-owned firms operated as sole proprietorships in 1972. Corporations were used least by black entrepreneurs as a legal form of organization.

Information shown in table 59 on total and black-owned firms (excluding corporations) indicates the extent of black gains relative to the total business market since 1969. Black firms in 1972 remained a marginal sector of the business community in every industry, accounting for about 2.7 percent of all businesses (excluding corporations) in the country, essentially the same proportion as in 1969. A very small increase was noted for gross receipts realized by black firms—1.7 percent of all gross receipts, slightly above the 1.3 percent in 1969.

In 1972, black-owned firms remained highly concentrated in two industry divisions—retail trade and selected services. These firms accounted for 65 percent of all black-owned firms, about the same proportion which existed in 1969. The category "selected services" includes hotels and other lodging places, personal services, business services, automotive repair services, garages, etc.

In terms of dollar volume of receipts among black-owned firms, automotive dealers (including service stations) and food stores ranked first and second.

The preponderance of black-owned firms operated in the South where there were 96,000 such businesses in 1972. However, the greatest percentage increases (1969 to 1972) were noted in the West and Northeast.

There were 16 States with 5,000 or more black-owned firms in 1972; about half were located outside the South. Three-fourths of the selected 16 States showed an increase of 50 percent or more in gross receipts since 1969. Very high increases (80 percent or more) were noted for Maryland, New York, District of Columbia, Florida, and California. In 1972, California recorded both the largest amount of gross receipts and number of firms of any State. Illinois, though second in rank for gross receipts, was fourth in number of firms; Texas was second in number of firms.

The seven standard metropolitan statistical areas having the largest number of black-owned firms in 1972 (5,000 or more) accounted for 31 percent of the total number of black-owned firms in the United States and 32 percent of gross receipts of all black-owned firms in the Nation. Gross receipts for the Chicago SMSA were substantially above those for any of the other 6 SMSA's.

BLACKS IN AMERICA

Table 11. Selected Characteristics of Black-Owned Firms: 1969 and 1972

(Minus sign (-) denotes decrease)

Selected characteristics	1969	1972	Percent change 1969 to 1972	Percent distribution	
				1969	1972
PRESENCE OF PAID EMPLOYEES AND GROSS RECEIPTS					
All firms......................	163,073	194,986	20	100	100
With paid employees...................	38,304	31,893	-17	23	16
Without paid employees...............	124,769	163,093	31	77	84
Average number of paid employees per firm................................	4	6	50	(X)	(X)
Gross receipts.............thousands..	$4,474,191	$7,168,491	60	(X)	(X)
Average receipts per firm...thousands..	$ 27.4	$ 36.8	34	(X)	(X)
LEGAL FORM OF ORGANIZATION					
All firms......................	163,073	194,986	20	100	100
Sole proprietorships...................	148,135	182,530	23	91	94
Partnerships..........................	11,424	8,422	-26	7	4
Corporations..........................	3,514	4,034	15	2	2
REGION OF LOCATION					
All firms[1]......................	162,050	192,861	19	100	100
South..................................	83,262	96,451	16	51	50
North and West........................	78,788	96,410	22	49	50
Northeast..........................	24,392	31,611	30	15	16
North Central.....................	36,635	41,400	13	23	21
West..................................	17,761	23,399	32	11	12

Note: Most of the data shown in tables 58 - 62 are from the 1972 and 1969 Surveys of Minority-Owned Businesses. A firm was considered to be black-owned if the sole owner or more than half of the partners were black. A corporation was classified as black-owned if more than 50 percent of the stock was owned by blacks. See "Definitions and Explanations" section for more details.

X Not applicable.
[1]Excludes 1,023 firms in 1969 and 2,125 firms in 1972 whose region of location was not reported.

Source: U.S. Department of Commerce, Social and Economic Statistics Administration, Bureau of the Census.

EDUCATION

School Enrollment

In 1974, about 700,000 black students were enrolled in nursery school and kindergarten and 4.6 million in elementary school (grades 1 to 8); another 2.1 million were in high school (grades 9 to 12) and 800,000 in college. Following the national trend, the number of black students enrolled at the elementary school level has declined since the beginning of the decade. This decline reflects the decrease in the elementary school-age population as the result of fewer births.

Between 1970 and 1974, there was a striking increase among blacks at the college level, where a 56 percent growth in enrollment was noted. For whites, the most dominant growth (about 50 percent) occurred at the nursery school level.

For both blacks and whites, nearly universal school enrollment still existed in 1974 at the compulsory attendance ages, 6 to 15 years. Also, for some age groups outside the compulsory attendance ages, the enrollment rates for black students have approximated those for whites. By 1974, the proportion of 5-year old black children enrolled was 87 percent, about the same level as that for whites (90 percent). Just 4 years ago, the figure for blacks had lagged below that for whites by at least 9 percentage points. The gains by blacks may be due, in part, to the increased availability of kindergarten to blacks since more public education systems, especially those in the South, have included kindergarten. In addition, among those 16 to 17 years of age, the proportion attending school was about the same for blacks and whites—about 88 percent.

Within the last 4 years, the college enrollment rates for young black men have continued to climb, whereas those for black women appear to have leveled off. Consequently, in 1974 there is some evidence that a higher proportion of young black men than women were enrolled in college—20 compared with 16 percent, respectively.

For both blacks and whites, college attendance for young adults (18 to 24 years old) tends to increase with family income.[1] However, at the $10,000 and over income level, a higher proportion of white than black families (with (a) family member (s) 18 to 24 years old) had a member enrolled in college—45 and 33 percent, respectively. Among families with incomes under $5,000, about the same proportion of black and white families (17 percent) had at least one member enrolled in college.

---

[1] Income data are based on respondent's estimate of total family money income received for the preceding 12 months and excludes families for whom no income information was obtained. Consequently, the income levels may be understated compared with income data collected from the March CPS, which are based on responses to eight direct questions asked of all persons and include allocation for nonresponse.

Table 12. School Enrollment of Persons 3 to 34 Years Old, by Level: 1970 and 1974

(Numbers in thousands. Minus sign (-) denotes decrease)

Level of school and race	1970	1974	Percent change, 1970 to 1974
BLACK			
Total enrolled	7,307	8,215	12.4
Nursery school	178	227	27.5
Kindergarten	426	463	8.7
Elementary school	4,868	4,585	-5.8
High school	1,834	2,125	15.9
College	522	814	55.9
WHITE			
Total enrolled	44,960	50,992	13.4
Nursery school	893	1,340	50.1
Kindergarten	2,706	2,745	1.4
Elementary school	28,638	26,051	-9.0
High school	12,723	13,073	2.8
College	6,759	7,781	15.1

Source: U.S. Department of Commerce, Social and Economic Statistics Administration, Bureau of the Census.

Table 13. Percent Enrolled in School, by Age: 1965, 1970, and 1974

Age	Black			White		
	1965	1970	1974	1965	1970	1974
3 and 4 years..................	[1]12	23	29	10	20	29
5 years........................	59	72	87	72	81	90
6 to 15 years..................	99	99	99	99	99	99
16 and 17 years................	84	86	87	88	91	88
18 and 19 years................	40	40	44	47	49	43
20 to 24 years.................	9	14	17	20	23	22

[1]Includes persons of "other" races.

Source: U.S. Department of Commerce, Social and Economic Statistics Administration, Bureau of the Census.

Table 14. College Enrollment of Persons 18 to 24 Years Old by Sex: 1970 and 1974

(Numbers in thousands)

Sex and college enrollment	Black		White	
	1970	1974	1970	1974
BOTH SEXES				
Total persons, 18 to 24 years......	2,692	3,105	19,608	22,141
Number enrolled in college..............	416	555	5,305	5,589
Percent of total......................	15	18	27	25
MALE				
Total persons, 18 to 24 years......	1,220	1,396	9,053	10,722
Number enrolled in college..............	192	280	3,096	3,035
Percent of total......................	16	20	34	28
FEMALE				
Total persons, 18 to 24 years......	1,471	1,709	10,555	11,419
Number enrolled in college..............	225	277	2,209	2,555
Percent of total......................	15	16	21	22

Source: U.S. Department of Commerce, Social and Economic Statistics Administration, Bureau of the Census.

Educational Attainment

Young blacks have continued to make advances in education in the 1970's. Moreover, the educational differentials between black and white young adults narrowed, continuing a pattern which began in the 1960's. The proportion of high school graduates rose faster for blacks than for whites between 1970 and 1974, narrowing the gap. Yet in 1974, there was still a noticeable difference between blacks and whites (20 to 24 years old) in the proportion completing high school—72 percent versus 85 percent, respectively.

Between 1970 and 1974, there is some evidence that black adults 25 to 34 years old continued to make gains in completing their college education. However, in 1974, the comparable proportion of white adult college graduates (21 percent) was about two and one-half times larger than the proportion for blacks (8 percent).

**Table 15. Level of Schooling Completed by Persons 20 to 24 Years Old,
by Sex: 1960, 1965, 1970, and 1974**

Level of schooling and year	Total		Male		Female	
	Black	White	Black	White	Black	White
Percent completed 4 years of high school or more:						
1960...............................	42	66	[1]39	65	[1]45	68
1965...............................	49	76	50	76	48	77
1970...............................	65	83	62	83	67	83
1974...............................	72	85	68	86	75	85
Percent completed 1 year of college or more:						
1960...............................	12	25	[1]12	28	[1]13	22
1965...............................	15	31	14	36	15	26
1970...............................	23	39	23	44	23	35
1974...............................	27	43	25	46	29	40

[1]Includes persons of "other" races.

Source: U.S. Department of Commerce, Social and Economic Statistics Administration, Bureau of the Census.

**Table 16. Percent of Population 25 to 34 Years Old Who Completed 4 Years of College or More,
by Sex: 1960, 1966, 1970, and 1974**

Year	Black			White		
	Total	Male	Female	Total	Male	Female
1960...........................	4.1	4.1	4.0	11.9	15.8	8.3
1966...........................	5.7	5.2	6.1	14.6	18.9	10.4
1970...........................	6.1	5.8	6.4	16.6	20.9	12.3
1974...........................	8.1	8.8	7.6	21.0	24.9	17.2

Source: U.S. Department of Commerce, Social and Economic Statistics Administration, Bureau of the Census.

Characteristics of Postsecondary Students

Nearly 680,000 blacks 16 to 34 years old were students in some type of postsecondary school in 1973, constituting about 9 percent of all blacks in that age span. For whites, the comparable figure was about 7.7 million, or about 14 percent of that age group.

The largest component (549,000) of black postsecondary students were enrolled in colleges or universities. Slightly more than 100,000 blacks were attending vocational schools, reported primarily as business or commercial, technical, and vocational or trade schools.

Selected data on students enrolled in postsecondary schools (i.e., schools providing training beyond high school) were collected as a supplement to the Census Bureau's October 1973 Current Population Survey (CPS).

Some differences between black and white enrollment by type of schooling were apparent. Black students were more likely than white students to be enrolled in vocational educational institutions and less likely to be in universities. On the other hand, the proportion of blacks enrolled in 4-year colleges (20 percent) was very similar to that for whites. However, black students were predominantly in public 4-year colleges, whereas white students were enrolled equally in public and private 4-year colleges.

Information on the financial status and sources of income of students also was gathered in this special CPS supplement. Contrary to general assumptions about the dependence of postsecondary students upon their parents, the majority of postsecondary students considered themselves financially independent of their parents.[2] This situation was also true for blacks—60 percent of the black students reported that they were financially independent. However, this independence among black students varied considerably by the type of school in which they were enrolled. For example, 78 percent of vocational school students, but only 47 percent of 4-year college students considered themselves financially independent. This pattern for blacks followed the same trend observed for all postsecondary students.

A larger proportion of black students who were dependent upon parental support than those who were financially independent were attending universities and 4-year colleges, where expenses are usually higher (median education expenses, excepted). This suggests that parental assistance enabled more of these black students to enroll at this higher level of schooling.

Postsecondary students used a number of sources of income to defray their educational and living expenses. However, most sources were used by only a small segment of the students. Among black students, the sources most often reported were personal earnings (40 percent), parents, and personal savings. Black students relied upon these sources to a lesser degree than all postsecondary students.

Generally, no loan, grant, or scholarship program, considered singly, affected a large proportion of all black students, but combined they affected a substantial number. And black students were more likely than all students to use all of these programs.

Among the grants and scholarships, the most common sources used by blacks were Educational Opportunity Grants,[3] Veterans Administration benefits, and State and local scholarships and grants. National Defense Student Loans were used to a greater extent than personal loans by black students.

---

[2] "Financially dependent" or "independent" is a self-determined status, i.e., based on the response of students to a question which asked directly if they considered themselves to be financially independent of their parents.

[3] The figure for Educational Opportunity Grants may not include all students who received grants in 1973, because the Basic Educational Opportunity Grant Program was begun in summer 1973 and many students were likely not to have been informed about their application until after the survey date.

Table 17. Postsecondary School Enrollment of Persons 16 to 34 Years Old, by Type of School: 1973

(Numbers in thousands)

Subject	All races	Black	White
PERSONS 16 TO 34 YEARS OLD			
Total...................................	61,546	7,152	53,464
Postsecondary students......................	8,524	678	7,659
Percent of total.....................	14	9	14
Enrolled in college........................	7,354	549	6,639
University...............................	4,032	252	3,698
4-year college...........................	1,570	134	1,386
2-year college...........................	1,752	163	1,555
Enrolled in vocational education school....	1,170	128	1,020
Postsecondary Students			
Total.............................	8,524	678	7,659
Percent..........................	100	100	100
Enrolled in college........................	86	81	87
University...............................	47	37	48
4-year college...........................	18	20	18
2-year college...........................	21	24	20
Enrolled in vocational education school......	14	19	13
College students, excluding university			
Total.............................	3,322	297	2,941
Percent..........................	100	100	100
Enrolled in 4-year college...................	47	45	47
Public...............................	25	36	23
Private..............................	21	8	23
Enrolled in 2-year college...................	53	55	53
Public...............................	48	47	48
Private..............................	3	5	3

Source: U.S. Department of Commerce, Social and Economic Statistics Administration, Bureau of the Census.

FAMILY

Structure and Composition

The proportion of black families with a husband and wife present continued its downward movement during the first half of the 1970 decade. In 1975, of the 5.5 million black families, about 61 percent had both spouses present; in 1970, the proportion was 68 percent. Conversely, the proportion of black families headed by a woman (with no spouse present) climbed from 28 to 35 percent. The proportion has been at about the 35 percent level for the last 3 years. White female heads as a percentage of all white families inched upward from 9 percent in 1970 to about 11 percent in 1975.

From the beginning of the decade to 1974, the number of black women who were heads of their own families increased by one-half million, or 37 percent; white female heads rose by nearly 700,000, or 16 percent. Some possible explanations for the rise in the total number of female family heads are suggested in a Census Bureau study. A few of the explanations cited are—high divorce and separation rates, the retention of children by unwed mothers, greater economic independence resulting from the increased incidence of labor force participation among women, and the availability of public assistance programs.[1] The influence of some of these factors is exhibited by changes which have occurred in the distribution of certain characteristics, namely the marital status, age, and the presence of children of female heads.

A greater proportion of black female family heads were either single or divorced (taken together) in 1974 than in 1970. This group has also increased faster than all black female heads. Furthermore, black women who were heads of families tended to be younger in 1974, on the average, than in 1970, as evidenced by the larger proportion who were under 35 years old—the increase was from 35 percent in 1970 to 40 percent in 1974. There is some evidence that more black female heads now have children to support—in 1974, about 70 percent of black female heads had children compared with 67 percent in 1970. Moreover, about 3.2 million black children were in families headed by women in 1974, compared with 2.6 million in 1970.

---

[1] See **Current Population Reports**, Series P-23, No. 50, "Female Family Heads," pages 1 and 2.

Table 18. Percent Distribution of Families by Type: 1965 and 1970 to 1975

Year and race	All families (thousands)	Percent of all families			
		Total	Husband-wife	Other male head	Female head[1]
BLACK					
1965[2]	4,752	100.0	73.1	3.2	23.7
1970	4,774	100.0	68.1	3.7	28.3
1971	4,928	100.0	65.6	3.8	30.6
1972[3]	5,157	100.0	63.8	4.4	31.8
1973[3]	5,265	100.0	61.4	4.0	34.6
1974[3]	5,440	100.0	61.8	4.2	34.0
1975[3]	5,498	100.0	60.9	3.9	35.3
WHITE					
1965	43,081	100.0	88.6	2.4	9.0
1970	46,022	100.0	88.7	2.3	9.1
1971	46,535	100.0	88.3	2.3	9.4
1972[3]	47,641	100.0	88.2	2.3	9.4
1973[3]	48,477	100.0	87.8	2.5	9.6
1974[3]	48,919	100.0	87.7	2.4	9.9
1975[3]	49,451	100.0	86.9	2.6	10.5

Note: Most of the tables in this section show data on families for the year 1974. Figures on families from the March 1975 Current Population Survey, which recently became available, have been included in this table in this section.

A family consists of two or more persons living together and related by blood, marriage, or adoption.

[1] Female heads of families include widowed, divorced, and single women, women whose husbands are in the Armed Forces or otherwise away from home involuntarily, as well as those separated from their husbands through marital discord.

[2] Includes persons of "other" races.

[3] Based on 1970 census population controls.

Source: U.S. Department of Commerce, Social and Economic Statistics Administration, Bureau of the Census.

Table 19. Marital Status of Female Family Heads: 1970 and 1974

(Numbers in thousands. Minus sign (-) denotes decrease)

Marital status and race	Number (thousands) 1970	Number (thousands) 1974	Percent change, 1970-1974	Percent distribution 1970	Percent distribution 1974
BLACK					
Total, female heads.......thousands..	1,349	1,849	37	100	100
With disrupted marriage....................	648	860	33	48	47
Separated................................	456	561	23	34	30
Divorced.................................	192	299	56	14	16
Other....................................	700	989	41	52	53
Single (never married)...................	218	389	78	16	21
Widowed..................................	403	536	33	30	29
Husband temporarily absent...............	79	64	-19	6	3
Armed Forces............................	31	10	-68	2	1
Other reasons...........................	48	54	13	4	3
WHITE					
Total, female heads.......thousands..	4,185	4,853	16	100	100
With disrupted marriage....................	1,534	2,273	48	37	47
Separated................................	476	715	50	11	15
Divorced.................................	1,058	1,558	47	25	32
Other....................................	2,651	2,580	-3	63	53
Single (never married)...................	385	454	18	9	9
Widowed..................................	1,966	1,925	-2	47	40
Husband temporarily absent...............	300	201	-33	7	4
Armed Forces............................	108	25	-77	3	1
Other reasons...........................	192	176	-8	5	4

Note: Categories refer to marital status at time of enumeration.

Source: U.S. Department of Commerce, Social and Economic Statistics Administration, Bureau of the Census.

FERTILITY

Fertility levels continued to fall in the 1970's. Between 1970 and 1973, total fertility rates declined at about the same pace for black and white women. In 1973, the rate was 2.44 children per black woman and 1.80 per white woman.

The drop in fertility levels for blacks is illustrated in figures on children already born to black women and on "expected" number of children. The average number of children ever born showed a decided drop among black women under 35 years of age. For example, all black women aged 30 to 34 years had borne an average of 2.5 children, a 17 percent drop from the level of 3.0 in 1970. On the other hand, the average number of children ever born among women 35 to 44 years of age in 1974 remained unchanged, but most of these women had completed their child-bearing years.

Black wives expect fewer children now than 4 years ago. Among black women 18 to 39 years old, the number of total births expected generally has declined since 1970.

There are no apparent differences in lifetime birth expectations between young blacks and whites; in 1974, both black and white women 18 to 24 years old expected an average of 2.2 children. However, since young black women have already had more births to date than the white women, they may not be successful in achieving their expressed expectations. Differentials in expectations between blacks and whites were still observable at ages above 25 years. Here too, black women have already had a larger number of children than white women.

Table 20. Total Fertility Rates: 1960 to 1974

Year	All races	Black and other races	Black	White
1960	3.65	4.52	(NA)	3.53
1961	3.63	4.53	(NA)	3.50
1962	3.47	[1]4.40	(NA)	[1]3.35
1963	3.33	[1]4.27	(NA)	[1]3.20
1964	3.21	4.15	(NA)	3.07
1965	2.93	3.89	(NA)	2.79
1966	2.74	3.61	3.58	2.61
1967	2.57	3.39	3.35	2.45
1968	2.48	3.20	3.13	2.37
1969	2.47	3.15	3.07	2.36
1970	2.48	3.07	3.10	2.39
1971	2.27	2.93	2.91	2.17
1972	2.02	2.65	2.62	1.92
1973	1.90	2.47	2.44	1.80
1974	[2]1.86	(NA)	(NA)	(NA)

Note: A total fertility rate is defined as the average number of births that each woman in a synthetic cohort of women would have in her lifetime if, at each year of age, the women experienced the birth rates occurring in the specified calendar year.

NA Not available.
[1]Excludes data for residents of New Jersey.
[2]Bureau of the Census estimate.

Source: U.S. Department of Health, Education, and Welfare, and U.S. Department of Commerce, Social and Economic Statistics Administration, Bureau of the Census.

HEALTH

Mortality

Life expectancy for blacks continues to be lower than that for whites.[1] Among blacks, the average life expectancy at birth in 1973 was 61.9 years for males and 70.1 years for females; corresponding figures for whites were 68.4 and 76.1. For both black males and females, life expectancy increased slightly more than 0.5 years between 1970 and 1973; for black males, this was an improvement over the 1960 decade when life expectancy remained unchanged.

The modest improvement in longevity for black persons in the 1970's reflects the drops which have occurred in the age-specific death rates. For example, over the 3-year period, 1970 to 1973, age-specific death rates for black females showed declines for most age groups. The most striking reduction occurred among the black population under 1 year of age—death rates declined by 19 percent for males and 16 percent for females.

Age-specific death rates in 1973 generally remained higher for blacks than for whites.

Death rates for most of the leading causes of death among black men and women showed modest to substantial declines during the first 3 years of the 1970's. Slight reductions were noted for major cardiovascular diseases (the leading cause of death) and accidents; the drops were especially pronounced for influenza and pneumonia (about 20 percent) and diseases associated with early infancy (about 28 percent). Among the exceptions to this pattern for blacks were malignant neoplasms (the second leading cause of death for both men and women) and homicide, a high ranking cause among the men, which registered increases between 1970 and 1973.

---

[1]In this section, the term "black" is used in the text although the data are for "black and other races." Blacks constitute about 90 percent of this group.

STATISTICAL DATA

157

Table 21. Life Expectancy at Selected Ages, by Sex: 1959-1961, 1970, and 1973

(Additional years of life expected)

Year and age	Male			Female		
	Black and other races	White	Difference in years of life	Black and other races	White	Difference in years of life
1959-61 [1]						
0 years (at birth)..........	61.5	67.6	-6.1	66.5	74.2	-7.7
1 year.....................	63.5	68.3	-4.8	68.1	74.7	-6.6
15 years...................	50.4	54.9	-4.5	54.9	61.2	-6.3
25 years...................	41.4	45.7	-4.3	45.4	51.5	-6.1
40 years...................	28.7	31.7	-3.0	32.2	37.1	-4.9
65 years...................	12.8	13.0	-0.2	15.1	15.9	-0.8
1970						
0 years (at birth)..........	61.3	68.0	-6.7	69.4	75.6	-6.2
1 year.....................	62.5	68.4	-5.9	70.4	75.8	-5.4
15 years...................	49.2	54.9	-5.7	57.0	62.2	-5.2
25 years...................	40.6	45.8	-5.2	47.5	52.5	-5.0
40 years...................	28.6	31.9	-3.3	34.2	38.3	-4.1
65 years...................	13.3	13.1	-0.2	16.4	17.1	-0.7
1973						
0 years (at birth)..........	61.9	68.4	-6.5	70.1	76.1	-6.0
1 years....................	62.8	68.6	-5.8	70.8	76.1	-5.3
15 years...................	49.5	55.1	-5.6	57.4	62.5	-5.1
25 years...................	40.8	46.0	-5.2	47.9	52.8	-4.9
40 years...................	28.7	32.2	-3.5	34.4	38.5	-4.1
65 years...................	13.1	13.2	-0.1	16.2	17.3	-1.1

[1] 3-year average.

Source: U.S. Department of Health, Education, and Welfare, National Center for Health Statistics.

Table 22. DEATHS AND DEATH RATES: 1930 TO 1972

[Rates are per 1,000 population for specified groups. Prior to 1960, excludes Alaska and Hawaii. Excludes fetal deaths. Population enumerated as of April 1 for 1940, 1950, 1960, and 1970, and estimated as of July 1 for all other years. Data prior to 1933 for death-registration States only; see text, p. 49. See also *Historical Statistics, Colonial Times to 1957*, series B 129-136]

ITEM	1930	1940	1950	1960	1965	1967	1968	1969	1970 [1]	1971 [1]	1972 [2]
Deaths..........1,000..	1,327	1,417	1,452	1,712	1,828	1,851	1,930	1,922	1,921	1,928	1,962
Male..............1,000..	727	791	828	976	1,035	1,046	1,087	1,081	1,078	1,077	1,095
Female............1,000..	601	626	625	736	793	805	843	841	843	850	867
White.............1,000..	1,137	1,231	1,276	1,505	1,605	1,627	1,690	1,684	1,682	1,690	1,721
Male..............	626	691	731	861	911	920	951	945	942	942	957
Female............	511	540	545	644	695	708	738	738	740	747	764
Negro and other...1,000..	190	186	176	207	223	224	241	238	239	238	241
Male..............	101	100	96	115	125	126	136	136	136	135	138
Female............	89	86	80	92	98	98	104	103	103	103	103
Death rates............	11.3	10.8	9.6	9.5	9.4	9.4	9.7	9.5	9.5	9.3	9.4
Male....................	12.3	12.0	11.1	11.0	10.9	10.8	11.1	11.0	10.9	10.7	10.8
Female..................	10.4	9.5	8.2	8.1	8.0	8.0	8.2	8.1	8.1	8.0	8.1
White...................	10.8	10.4	9.5	9.5	9.4	9.4	9.6	9.5	9.5	9.3	9.4
Male....................	11.7	11.6	10.9	11.0	10.8	10.8	11.1	10.9	10.9	10.7	10.8
Female..................	9.8	9.2	8.0	8.0	8.0	8.0	8.2	8.2	8.1	8.1	8.2
Negro and other.........	16.3	13.8	11.2	11.2	10.1	9.6	9.4	9.9	9.6	9.4	9.3
Male....................	17.4	15.1	12.5	11.5	11.1	10.9	11.6	11.3	11.2	10.8	11.1
Female..................	15.3	12.6	9.9	8.7	8.2	7.9	8.3	8.0	7.8	7.7	7.6
Age:											
Under 1 year...........	69.0	54.9	33.0	27.0	24.1	22.3	22.3	21.5	21.4	18.5	18.0
1-4 years..............	5.6	2.9	1.4	1.1	0.9	0.9	0.9	0.9	0.8	0.8	0.8
5-14 years.............	1.7	1.0	0.6	0.5	0.4	0.4	0.4	0.4	0.4	0.4	0.4
15-24 years............	3.3	2.0	1.3	1.1	1.1	1.2	1.2	1.3	1.3	1.3	1.3
25-34 years............	4.7	3.1	1.8	1.5	1.5	1.5	1.6	1.6	1.6	1.6	1.6
35-44 years............	6.8	5.2	3.6	3.0	3.1	3.1	3.2	3.2	3.1	3.1	3.0
45-54 years............	12.2	10.6	8.5	7.6	7.4	7.3	7.5	7.3	7.3	7.1	7.1
55-64 years............	24.0	22.2	19.0	17.4	16.9	16.7	17.2	16.8	16.6	16.3	16.1
65-74 years............	51.4	48.4	41.0	38.2	37.9	37.5	38.5	37.4	35.8	35.9	35.5
75-84 years............	112.7	112.0	93.3	87.5	81.9	79.0	80.8	79.0	80.0	77.5	79.0
85 years and over......	228.0	235.7	202.0	198.6	202.0	194.2	196.1	190.8	163.4	177.6	162.2

[1] Excludes nonresident alien deaths.   [2] Preliminary. Based on a 10-percent sample of deaths.

Source: U.S. National Center for Health Statistics, *Vital Statistics of the United States*, annual, and unpublished data.

VOTING

Voting and Registration

About one-third of the black American electorate reported that they voted in the congressional election of 1974. This turnout was about 10 percentage points lower than the 1970 congressional election and 18 percentage points lower than the 1972 Presidential election. Similar declines in voter participation were noted for whites; by 1974, the overall voting participation rate was at a low of 46 percent.

The pattern of lower voter turnout for blacks in 1974 than in 1970 prevailed in all sections of the country. However, the decline was greater in the North and West (13 percentage points).

Among both blacks and whites, voter participation varied by age. The voter participation rate in 1974 was lowest for youth 18 to 24 years old (about 1 out of 6 black youth and 1 out of 4 white youth). Persons 45 to 64 years of age were more likely than those in any other age group to have voted—46 percent for blacks and 58 percent for whites.

Among the total population, high levels of voter participation are associated with high educational attainment. The pattern, though evident, was not as strong for blacks as for whites in 1974. About one-half of black college graduates reported voting in 1974, compared with about one-third of those who had completed only high school. However, voter turnout for those who had completed high school was no greater than that for persons with only an elementary school education.

Registration rates for blacks in 1974 were at the lowest level reported for any of the last five general elections. (The Census Bureau first collected data on voter registration for the election of 1966.) In 1974, about 55 percent of the black electorate was registered to vote; for the previous four elections (1966 to 1972), the levels had ranged from 61 to 66 percent.

Between the congressional elections of 1970 and 1974, registration rates declined about 6 percentage points for blacks. The drop observed for blacks at the national level was the result, primarily, of the steep decline in the North and West where the rate dipped from 65 percent in 1970 to 54 percent in 1974. The registration rate for blacks living in the South was not statistically different in 1974 than in 1970.

Among the 2.6 million blacks who were registered but did not vote in the 1974 congressional election, about 45 percent indicated that they had been "unable to go to the polls." A lower proportion (33 percent) of the whites had given this reason for not voting. The category "unable to go to the polls" included reasons such as "illness and disability," "family emergency," "could't leave work, " or "couldn't get to the polls." About one-fifth of both blacks and whites reported they were not interested as their primary reason for not voting. Reasons such as "out of town or away from home" and "dislikes politics" were more frequently reported by whites than by blacks.

Among the 5.2 million blacks who were not registered in 1974, nearly one-half reported that they were not interested or disliked politics.

Table 23. WHITE AND NEGRO VOTER REGISTRATION IN 11 SOUTHERN STATES: 1960 TO 1971

[In thousands, except percent. For 1960 to 1970 covers population 18 years old and over in Georgia, and 21 and over elsewhere; for 1971, covers population 18 years old and over for all the Southern States. For voting age population, see table 705]

ITEM	Total	Ala.	Ark.	Fla.	Ga.	La.	Miss.	N.C.	S.C.	Tenn.	Tex.	Va.
1960: White	12,276	860	518	1,819	1,020	993	478	1,861	481	1,300	2,079	867
Negro	1,463	66	73	183	180	159	22	210	58	185	227	100
Percent white [1] [2]	61.1	63.6	60.9	69.3	56.8	76.9	63.9	92.1	57.1	73.0	42.5	46.1
Percent negro [1] [2]	29.1	13.7	38.0	39.4	29.3	31.1	5.2	39.1	13.7	59.1	35.5	23.1
1964: White	14,264	948	621	2,200	1,340	1,037	525	1,942	703	1,297	2,602	1,050
Negro	2,164	111	95	300	270	165	29	258	144	218	375	200
1966: White	14,310	1,192	598	2,093	1,378	1,072	471	1,654	718	1,375	2,600	1,159
Negro	2,689	250	115	303	300	243	175	282	191	225	400	205
1968: White	15,702	1,117	640	2,195	1,524	1,133	691	1,579	587	1,448	3,582	1,256
Negro	3,112	273	130	292	344	305	251	305	189	228	540	255
1970: White	16,985	1,311	728	2,495	1,615	1,143	690	1,640	668	1,600	3,599	1,496
Negro	3,357	315	153	302	395	319	286	305	221	242	550	269
1971: White	17,378	1,370	674	[3]3,018	1,598	[3]1,388	671	[3]1,970	[3]773	1,542	3,700	1,550
Negro	3,449	290	165	[3]351	450	[3]397	268	[3]388	[3]261	245	575	275
Percent white [1] [2]	65.0	78.5	61.4	[3]86.6	68.8	[3]77.7	69.7	[3]83.6	[3]74.7	67.3	56.8	59.6
Percent negro [1] [2]	58.6	54.7	80.9	[3]13.4	64.2	[3]22.3	59.4	[3]16.4	[3]25.3	65.6	68.2	52.0

[1] Of voting age population.   [2] Includes other minority races.   [3] 1972 data.

Source: Voter Educaton Project, Inc., Atlanta, Ga., *Voter Registration in the South.*

Table 24. Reported Voter Participation of Persons of Voting Age, by Region: 1968, 1970, 1972, and 1974

(Numbers in thousands)

Subject	Congressional election		Presidential election	
	1970	1974	1968	1972
BLACK				
Number who reported that they voted:				
United States..........................	4,992	4,786	6,300	7,033
South.................................	2,278	2,219	3,094	3,324
North and West........................	2,714	2,567	3,206	3,707
Percent of voting-age population who reported that they voted:				
United States..........................	44	34	58	52
South.,...............................	37	30	52	48
North and West........................	51	38	65	57
Percent of registered population who reported that they voted:				
United States..........................	72	62	87	80
South.................................	64	54	84	75
North and West........................	80	70	90	85
WHITE				
Number who reported that they voted:				
United States..........................	60,426	57,918	72,213	78,167
South.................................	14,313	13,850	17,853	20,201
North and West........................	46,113	44,069	54,362	57,966
Percent of voting-age population who reported that they voted:				
United States..........................	56	46	69	64
South.................................	46	37	62	57
North and West........................	60	50	72	68
Percent of registered population who reported that they voted:				
United States..........................	81	73	92	88
South.................................	71	61	87	82
North and West........................	84	77	93	90

Source: U.S. Department of Commerce, Social and Economic Statistics Administration, Bureau of the Census.

ELECTED OFFICIALS

The number of blacks elected to office has continued the tremendous surge which began in the mid-1960's. In May 1975, 3,503 blacks were holding office, a marked increase (88 percent) over the March 1971 figure of 1,860.

The increase since 1971 in black elected officials has been most predominant in the Southern region. The South, which contains 53 percent of the black population in the United States, now accounts for 55 percent of all elected black officials. Forty-four percent of black State legislators and executives and 61 percent of the black mayors were in the South.

The largest number of blacks holding office were found in Illinois and Louisiana, two States which registered the largest numerical increases in black elected officials during the last year. Sixteen States, one-half of which are in the South, have more than 100 black officeholders.

Major advancements reflecting the results of the most recent congressional elections (1974) include one new member in Congress and 42 additional State legislators and executives, including 2 Lieutenant Governors. The State legislatures of at least three Southern States—Alabama, Georgia, and South Carolina—have more black members than at any other time since Reconstruction.[1]

There were 135 black mayors in 1975, a 67 percent increase from 1971. Blacks are now the mayors of 11 large metropolitan cities (population of 100,000 or more; 2 of which—Los Angeles and Detroit—have populations of over 1 million). Black mayors govern primarily small towns and communities—104 black mayors headed communities with fewer than 25,000 residents and of these 51 were mayors of places with total populations of under 1,000. The majority of black mayors were holding office in towns and places which are predominantly black, i.e., blacks were at least 50 percent of the population.

Since 1969, the number of black women holding public office has quadrupled —from 131 to 530—but their proportion of all black officeholders has increased only slightly to 15 percent.

Traditionally, few women have been elected mayors, State legislators and executives, or U. S. Congresswomen. Some changes in this pattern are apparent—in 1975 there were 9 black women mayors and 35 State legislators. However, most of the women still hold positions in educational fields and at the municipal level.

---

[1] Focus, Joint Center for Political Studies, Vol. 3, No. 1.

Table 25. Black Elected Officials, by Type of Office: 1964, 1971, 1973, and 1975

Office and area	1964	1971	1973	1975
Total......................	103	1,860	2,621	3,503
United States Senators:				
United States..................	-	1	1	1
South.........................	-	-	-	-
House of Representatives:				
United States..................	5	13	15	17
South.........................	-	2	4	5
State legislators and executives:				
United States..................	94	198	240	281
South.........................	16	70	90	124
Mayors:				
United States..................	(NA)	81	82	135
South.........................	(NA)	47	48	82
Other:[1]				
United States..................	(NA)	1,567	2,283	3,069
South.........................	(NA)	763	1,239	1,702

Note: Figures for 1964 represent the total number of elected blacks holding office at that time, not just those elected in that year. The 1971, 1973, and 1975 figures represent the number of elected blacks holding office as of the end of March 1971, March 1973, and May 1975, respectively.

- Represents zero.   NA Not available.
[1]Includes all black elected officials not included in first four categories.

Source: Joint Center for Political Studies; Potomac Institute, et al (1964 data).

ARMED FORCES

As of June 1974, about 300,000 black men and women were serving in the Armed Forces of this country. The number of blacks in the Armed Forces has shown virtually no change since 1970, whereas the total Armed Forces has declined substantially. Thus, blacks comprised a greater share of the Armed Forces in 1974 than in 1970—14 percent compared to 10 percent. In the 1970's the proportion of blacks increased in all four branches of the Armed Forces. In 1974, the percent black ranged from 8 percent for the Navy to 19 percent for the Army.

Blacks represented 3 percent of all officers in the Armed Forces in 1974 but 16 percent of the enlisted persons. Among the four branches of the Armed Forces, the highest proportion of black officers (5 percent) was for the Army.

Black Armed Forces personnel had educational levels similar to those of all Armed Forces, although a slightly smaller proportion of blacks had completed high school or were college graduates. For example, in 1974, about 75 percent of the black enlisted personnel had finished high school; the comparable proportion among all service persons was 79 percent. Of the 9,000 black officers, 77 percent were college graduates; the corresponding figure was 81 percent for all officers.

Table 26. Officer-Enlisted Status of Armed Forces Personnel, by Type of Service: 1970 and 1974

(Numbers in thousands)

Military service and status	Total 1970	Total 1974	Black 1970	Black 1974	Percent black 1970	Percent black 1974
All services, total...........	2,861	2,151	279	298	9.8	13.8
Officer.........................	389	302	8	9	2.2	2.8
Enlisted........................	2,472	1,848	271	289	11.0	15.7
Army..........................	1,230	780	149	148	12.1	19.0
Officer.........................	160	106	5	5	3.4	4.5
Enlisted........................	1,069	674	144	143	13.5	21.3
Navy..........................	645	542	31	41	4.8	7.5
Officer.........................	78	67	1	1	0.7	1.3
Enlisted........................	567	475	30	40	5.4	8.4
Marine Corps....................	232	189	24	31	10.2	16.5
Officer.........................	23	19	-	-	1.3	2.4
Enlisted........................	209	170	23	31	11.2	18.1
Air Force.......................	755	640	75	78	10.0	12.1
Officer.........................	128	111	2	2	1.7	2.2
Enlisted........................	627	529	73	75	11.7	14.2

Note: Figures for 1970 represent the total number of officers and enlisted personnel as of December 1970; figures for 1974 are as of June 1974.

\- Rounds to zero.

Source: U.S. Department of Defense.

Table 27. NEGRO MEN IN THE ARMED FORCES: 1965 TO 1973

[In thousands, except percent. As of December 31]

YEAR AND ITEM	Total	Offi-cers[1]	En-listed men	PARTICIPATION IN VIETNAM[2] Total	Army	Navy[3]	Marine Corps	Air Force	Vietnam battle deaths since 1961
1965, Armed Forces..........	2,843	338	2,505	184	117	8	38	21	2
Negro....................	269	6	263	22	17	(Z)	4	1	(Z)
Percent of total...........	9.5	1.9	10.5	12.0	14.5	5.1	10.5	4.8	14.6
1967, Armed Forces..........	3,384	402	2,982	486	320	32	78	56	16
Negro....................	303	8	295	48	35	1	6	6	2
Percent of total...........	8.9	2.1	9.9	9.8	11.1	4.7	8.2	10.5	14.1
1968, Armed Forces..........	3,395	418	2,977	848	383	252	157	56	31
Negro....................	313	9	304	75	42	13	14	6	4
Percent of total...........	9.2	2.1	10.2	8.8	11.1	5.0	8.8	10.0	13.5
1969, Armed Forces..........	3,285	408	2,877	453	235	91	60	67	40
Negro....................	286	9	277	40	21	5	7	7	5
Percent of total...........	8.7	2.1	9.6	8.9	9.2	5.2	12.3	10.1	12.9
1970, Armed Forces..........	2,861	389	2,472	378	227	53	40	58	44
Negro....................	279	8	271	43	29	3	8	8	6
Percent of total...........	9.8	2.2	11.0	11.5	12.7	5.1	8.9	14.4	12.5
1971, Armed Forces..........	2,505	350	2,146	237	109	88	5	35	45
Negro....................	267	8	259	23	13	4	1	5	6
Percent of total...........	10.7	2.3	12.1	9.5	11.7	4.9	12.8	13.7	12.4
1972, Armed Forces..........	2,335	329	2,006	128	13	97	5	13	46
Negro....................	278	8	270	11	2	7	(Z)	2	6
Percent of total...........	11.9	2.4	13.5	8.7	12.4	7.5	8.8	13.9	12.3
1973, Armed Forces..........	2,189	308	1,881	(Z)	(Z)	(Z)	(Z)	(Z)	46
Negro....................	287	8	279	(Z)	(Z)	(Z)	(Z)	(Z)	6
Percent of total...........	13.1	2.6	14.8	(Z)	(Z)	(Z)	(Z)	(Z)	12.3

Z Less than 500 or 0.05 percent.   [1] Includes warrant officers.   [2] Beginning 1968, includes offshore.
[3] Includes Coast Guard.

CRIME: VICTIMS AND OFFENDERS

Criminal Victimization

During 1973, crimes of violence and common theft, including attempts, accounted for 2.3 million victimizations against black persons and 18.2 million victimizations against white persons, 12 years old and over. Information on criminal victimization in 1973 was gathered from surveys of a National Crime Panel.

The 1973 study indicated that the victimization rate of 132 per 1,000 blacks 12 years old and over was not significantly different from the 127 rate for whites.[1] This was a change from studies conducted in the 1960's which had shown that blacks were more likely than whites to be victims of crime[2].

An analysis of the variables associated with the likelihood of being victimized reveals both similarities and differences between the black and white populations. Victimization rates for both racial groups were generally higher among the male, and there was some evidence that the rate for black males was higher than that for white males. However, no difference exists between the rates for black and white females, which were the lowest.

Among both races, high victimization rates were associated with teenagers (12 to 19 years) and young adults (20 to 34 years), with the rate for white teenagers being the most pronounced.

Among the measured offenses, crimes of theft (personal larceny) were most frequently reported in the survey, and accounted for about 64 percent of all the criminal acts against black persons and 75 percent of those against whites. Of the three specific personal crimes of violence, assault was the most common and rape was the least frequently reported for both racial groups.

Blacks were much more likely than whites to have been the victims of violent crimes; the victimization rate was 47 per 1,000 population for blacks compared with 32 for whites. Regardless of the sex or age category, the rates for crimes of violence were generally more prevalent among blacks than among whites.

Among blacks, victimization rates for crimes of violence tended to vary with the income level. For persons in families with income under $10,000 (shown in table 108), the rate for crimes of violence declined as the income levels rose. On the other hand, the rate for blacks with family income of $15,000 and over was not statistically different than for those in the $7,500 to $9,999 income category.

Past studies have shown that black persons are more often attacked by blacks and white persons by whites.[3] The 1973 data on victimizations committed by a single offender tend to support these findings. About 87 percent of victimizations involving black victims were committed by a black; about 74 percent of the victimizations against whites were by a white assailant.

Approximately, 5 out of 10 black victimizations (excluding personal larceny without contact) involving only a lone assailant were committed by a person known to the victim (not a stranger). The corresponding proportion was slightly lower for whites—4 out of 10. Also, for crimes of violence, black victims were more likely than the comparable group of whites to be attacked by a person known to the victim—family members or acquaintances.

Previous surveys have indicated that crime is underreported to law enforcement authorities.[4] According to the 1973 survey, about one-half of the victimizations were not reported to the police by either black or white victims.

---

[1] The victimization rate for crimes against persons is a measure of occurrence among population groups at risk and is computed on the basis of the number of victimizations per 1,000 population age 12 and over.
[2] **Criminal Victimization in the United States,** National Opinion Research Center, p. 36 and "Crimes of Violence," a staff report to the National Commission of Causes and Prevention of Violence.
[3] Ibid.
[4] **Criminal Victimization in the United States,** National Opinion Research Center, pp. 41-50.

Table 28. Number and Rate of Personal Victimizations, by Type of Crime: 1973

Race of victim and type of crime	Victimizations		Victimization rate[1]
	Number (thousands)	Percent	
BLACK			
Total.....................	2,255	100	132
Crimes of violence.....................	801	36	47
Rape and attempted rape...............	29	1	2
Robbery and attempted robbery.........	245	11	14
Assault and attempted assault.........	527	23	31
Crimes of theft.......................	1,454	64	85
Personal larceny with contact.........	118	5	7
Personal larceny without contact......	1,336	59	78
WHITE			
Total.....................	18,211	100	127
Crimes of violence.....................	4,642	25	32
Rape and attempted rape...............	129	1	1
Robbery and attempted robbery.........	856	5	6
Assault and attempted assault.........	3,657	20	26
Crimes of theft.......................	13,569	75	95
Personal larceny with contact.........	381	2	3
Personal larceny without contact......	13,188	72	92

Note: Data in tables 106 to 111 on criminal victimization in 1973 were gathered from surveys of a National Crime Panel, conducted by the Bureau of the Census. The surveys were sponsored by the Department of Justice, Law Enforcement Assistance Administration.

[1]The victimization rate, a measure of occurrence among population groups at risk, was computed on the basis of the number of victimizations per 1,000 population age 12 and over.

Source: U.S. Department of Justice, Law Enforcement Assistance Administration.

Table 29. HOMICIDE VICTIMS AND SUICIDES, BY RACE AND SEX: 1930 TO 1972

YEAR	HOMICIDE VICTIMS					SUICIDES				
	Total	White		Negro and other		Total	White		Negro and other	
		Male	Female	Male	Female		Male	Female	Male	Female
NUMBER										
1930	[1]10,331	[1]4,605	[1]1,236	[1]3,628	[1]862	18,323	13,877	3,863	442	141
1935	[1]10,396	[1]4,200	[1]1,116	[1]4,167	[1]913	18,214	13,465	4,094	477	178
1940	8,329	2,977	796	3,670	886	18,907	13,990	4,294	476	147
1945	7,547	2,759	791	3,210	787	14,782	10,374	3,920	380	108
1950	7,942	2,586	952	3,503	901	17,145	12,755	3,713	542	135
1955	7,418	2,439	922	3,191	866	16,760	12,430	3,662	531	137
1960	8,464	2,832	1,154	3,437	1,041	19,041	13,825	4,296	714	206
1965	10,712	3,660	1,379	4,488	1,185	21,507	14,624	5,718	866	299
1968	14,686	5,106	1,700	6,417	1,463	21,372	14,520	5,692	859	301
1969	15,477	5,215	1,801	6,951	1,510	22,364	14,886	6,152	971	355
1970 [2]	16,848	5,865	1,938	7,413	1,632	23,480	15,591	6,468	1,038	383
1971	18,787	6,455	2,106	8,357	1,869	24,092	15,802	6,775	1,058	457
1972 (prel.)	18,880	6,740	2,150	8,250	1,740	24,280	15,990	6,670	1,300	310
RATE [3]										
1930	[1]12.4	[1]12.1	[1]3.3	[1]92.6	[1]21.8	22.1	36.4	10.4	11.3	3.6
1935	[1]11.2	[1]9.9	[1]2.7	[1]94.4	[1]20.2	19.6	31.8	9.8	10.8	3.9
1940	8.4	6.7	1.8	79.9	18.5	19.2	31.3	9.6	10.4	3.1
1945	7.7	6.8	1.7	71.4	15.2	15.1	25.6	8.2	8.5	2.1
1950	7.2	5.3	1.9	67.4	16.2	15.6	26.0	7.4	10.4	2.4
1955	6.4	4.8	1.7	57.8	14.4	14.5	24.5	6.9	9.6	2.3
1960	6.9	5.3	2.0	56.2	15.6	15.4	25.7	7.6	11.7	3.1
1965	8.0	6.3	2.2	66.6	15.9	16.1	25.3	9.2	12.0	4.0
1968	10.5	8.5	2.6	90.0	18.2	15.2	24.2	8.8	12.1	3.8
1969	10.9	8.6	2.7	95.1	18.3	15.7	24.4	9.3	13.3	4.3
1970 [2]	11.6	9.5	2.9	95.9	18.5	16.2	25.3	9.6	13.4	4.3
1971	12.7	10.2	3.1	107.8	21.4	16.3	25.0	9.9	13.6	5.2
1972 ((prel.)	12.5	10.4	3.1	103.3	19.1	16.0	24.8	9.6	16.3	3.4

[1] Excludes legal executions. [2] Excludes non-resident deaths. [3] Per 100,000 resident population 15 years old and over; enumerated as of April 1 for 1930, 1940, 1950, 1960, and 1970; estimated as of July 1 for all other years.

Source: U.S. National Center for Health Statistics, *Vital Statistics of the United States*, annual.

NAME INDEX

NAME INDEX